COP   7

YA796.357
   Thorn, John, 1947-
      Baseball's 10 greatest games / by
   John Thorn. New York : Four Winds
   Press, c1981.
      p. cm.
      Describes, inning by inning, the key
   plays and players of 10 classic baseball
   games from 1907 to 1967.
      ISBN 0-590-07665-5   RCN 0-590-07665-5
      1. Baseball--United States--History--
   Juvenile literature. 2. Baseball--
   History. I. Title.
      GV863.A1   796.357   80-66251

General Research Corp.   1981

BASEBALL'S
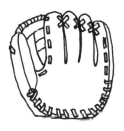
⚾ 10 ⚾
GREATEST GAMES

BY JOHN THORN

Foreword by Tom Seaver

FOUR WINDS PRESS
NEW YORK

ALSO BY JOHN THORN

A Century of Baseball Lore
The Relief Pitcher

LIBRARY OF CONGRESS CATALOGING IN PUBLICATION DATA

Thorn, John [date].
   Baseball's ten greatest games.

   SUMMARY: Describes, inning by inning, the key plays
and players of 10 classic baseball games from 1907 to
1978.
   1. Baseball—United States—History—Juvenile
literature. [1. Baseball—History] I. Title.
GV863.A1T46   796.357   80–66251
ISBN 0–590–07665–5

Published by Four Winds Press
A division of Scholastic Inc., New York, N.Y.
Copyright © 1981 by John Thorn
All rights reserved
Printed in the United States of America
Library of Congress Catalog Card Number: 80–66251
Book design by Constance Ftera
1 2 3 4 5 85 84 83 82 81

For Rick and Brian

Acknowledgments

For help in tracking down the countless small details which bring my ten games to life, I thank:

The men who played in these games and who, even more than half a century later, fondly recalled the events to me as clearly as if the games had been played yesterday.

The National Baseball Hall of Fame and Museum, in particular its librarian, Jack Redding, who as always was unfailingly cooperative and extravagantly tolerant.

The staffs of the public libraries whose research facilities I used, namely those of New York, Cincinnati, Milwaukee, Chicago, and Saugerties, my home town.

The public-relations directors of the major-league clubs which were involved in these ten games, with special thanks to Hal Middlesworth, recently retired as p.r. director of the Detroit Tigers.

Helen Marks, who ferreted out some vital facts about the 1917 classic just as this book was entering production.

Barbara Violante, of the Chicago Historical Society, who unearthed invaluable material about that 1917 game.

And for other sorts of help along the way, thanks to:

David Reuther, my editor and friend.

Beverly Reingold, whose encouragement prompted me to try my hand at writing for young people.

And, of course, my family: my parents, who have put up with my baseball mania all these years; my son, now three and a half, who, just to be supportive, assures me that he likes baseball better than golf; and my wife, who sustains me in everything I do.

Contents

Foreword by Tom Seaver   1

Introduction   3

1 September 30, 1907:
   Detroit Tigers vs. Philadelphia A's   7

2 May 2, 1917:
   Cincinnati Reds vs. Chicago Cubs   25

3 October 10, 1924:
   New York Giants vs. Washington Senators   43

4 October 12, 1929:
   Chicago Cubs vs. Philadelphia A's   61

5 October 3, 1951:
   Brooklyn Dodgers vs. New York Giants   77

6 October 8, 1956:
   Brooklyn Dodgers vs. New York Yankees   97

7 May 26, 1959:
   Pittsburgh Pirates vs. Milwaukee Braves   115

8 October 13, 1960:
   New York Yankees vs. Pittsburgh Pirates   133

9 October 21, 1975:
   Cincinnati Reds vs. Boston Red Sox   153

10 October 2, 1978:
   New York Yankees vs. Boston Red Sox   173

Afterword   193

Index   195

Foreword

It's funny how baseball writers and fans alike have a way of boiling down a memorable ball game into one crucial play. Over the years, many people have said to me, "I was there the night you lost your perfect game in the ninth." They remember that Jimmy Qualls of the Cubs looped a single to left-center to break the spell. But do they know how the previous batter was retired, or who the opposing pitcher was, or how the Mets backed me up in the field? Like all baseball games, my "almost perfect game" had a beginning and a middle, as well as an end.

That's one of the reasons I found BASEBALL'S TEN GREATEST GAMES uniquely satisfying, one of the best baseball books I've ever read. John Thorn has captured something I've never felt in a book before—the *rhythm* of the game. He puts you in the ballpark, so that you can see for yourself the clutch hits, the bad hops, the manager's strategies, the pitching patterns that all lead up to those explosive, unforgettable conclusions. We see that famous final-inning home runs—by Bobby Thomson, or Bill Mazeroski, or Carlton Fisk—don't tell the whole story of those great games, and that Walter Johnson, Don Larsen, and Harvey Haddix couldn't have achieved their incredible pitching performances without help from their teammates.

There's one more very important feature of a great baseball game that I'm happy to see included. There is no thrill like that of throwing a no-hitter, making a one-in-a-million catch, or knocking in a World Series winning run. But in baseball, the joy of one player is often the heartbreak of another. For every Bobby Thomson there is a Ralph Branca, for every Fred Toney, a Hippo Vaughn. There are two sides to every game, and this book gives the human element of each side its due.

Great games are the monuments of baseball's history, but as the years go by, they become frozen in time and place. In the pages ahead, John Thorn brings these ten greatest of great games to life. I know you'll enjoy them as much as I did.

TOM SEAVER

Introduction

What's the best baseball game you ever saw? Was it a pitchers' duel, closely fought and decided by a solitary run in the late innings; or a batters' brawl, with huge leads swinging back and forth? Or was it a contest in which a player, perhaps your favorite, did something unexpected and splendid? No matter what sort of game it was, chances are that the team you were rooting for won, and that you were thrilled in a way you will always remember.

For me, the best game was a 5–0 win by the Brooklyn Dodgers over the New York Giants at the Polo Grounds when I was a boy. It was the first time I ever set foot in a ball park, my father bought me hot dogs and peanuts, and Duke Snider belted a homer. It was a perfect day, a wonderful memory . . . but a *great* game? No. The Dodgers scored early, Johnny Podres toyed with the Giant batters, and my hero's home run was a late, meaningless tally in a game unremarkable to everyone but me.

So what makes a game "great"? And how, from the more than 125,000 major-league games that have been played, can anyone select a mere ten? For though all baseball games are significantly different, they are also essentially alike. In absolutely every contest, something happens that can fairly be called "great": a dazzling grab, a clutch hit, masterful pitching with men on base. Yet not many contests can be called great as a whole.

The great game has some generally agreed-upon characteristics. A close game played in the fall will mean more than one played in the summer (though not in the standings), and a well-played game between pennant contenders will be superior to one between tailenders. Also, an individual performance that rewrites the record books does not by itself make for an exceptional game. For example, Reggie Jackson's three home runs on three consecutive pitches in the finale of the 1977 World Series will not soon be forgotten, but the game has already begun to fade from memory. That's because the final score was Yankees 8, Dodgers 4, and all but two of the game's twelve runs crossed the plate in the first five frames. The outcome of a great contest must be in doubt till the end. Like classic drama, the great game is great in more than its details. It requires a proper setting, a worthy cast of characters, an exquisite suspense, a stunning reversal, and, in the end, a satisfaction that goes beyond mere victory or defeat.

When a game is truly special, both the participants and the spectators share in the honor of having been there. In the eleventh inning of Game Six of the 1975 World Series, Cincinnati's Pete Rose turned in the batter's box to face Carlton Fisk, the Boston catcher. "Some kind of game, isn't it?" he said. After the game, which Fisk won with a homer in the next inning, Rose declared that the game was "the greatest I've ever played in, absolutely the greatest. I'm just proud to be part of the game."

Ralph Branca, who on October 3, 1951, before 34,320 lucky fans, threw the single most famous pitch in baseball history, has said: "Whenever somebody tells me he was there I tell him he's the four-hundred-and-thirty-first thousandth guy to tell me he was at the game."

Of course, in the age of television the audience for a baseball game is no longer limited to the seating capacity of the park. For Game Six of the '75 Series, 62 million people could say, "I was there." You may have been one of them. But technology cannot enable us to step back in time and witness games whose glories passed uncaptured on film, yet which have endured and taken their place in baseball lore. Nor will snippets of more recent games, stitched together into a "highlights" program, call up the excitement of seeing the game unfold as it was happening.

If I can take you back with me to those old ball parks, those fabled games, those storied players, perhaps you will "see" Ty Cobb square off against Rube Waddell, or Jim Thorpe drive in the only run of a double no-hit game, or old Walter Johnson finally win in the World Series. And I'd like you to experience Bobby Thomson's "shot heard 'round the world," and Harvey Haddix's heartbreak loss, and Bucky Dent's moment in the sun, and more. My fondest wish is that when we've finished our look back on baseball's ten greatest games, you'll feel that you can say, "I was there."

JOHN THORN
Saugerties, New York

September 30, 1907
Detroit Tigers
vs.
Philadelphia A's

Game time is two o'clock, sixty minutes from now, but the 18,000 seats in Philadelphia's Columbia Park were filled hours ago and the gates have just been closed. You and I were fortunate to squeeze into the standing-room section roped off here on the center-field grass. A seat in the grandstand or bleachers would have been nicer, I know, but we mustn't complain: at least we gained admission, unlike the swarms of disgruntled fans milling outside the fences, and the thousands who risk their necks on the rooftops of houses which overlook this rickety wooden stadium.

7

Who would have imagined that a Monday date with the Detroit Tigers, perennial also-rans, could produce such a crush of humanity? Two years back, when the A's fought the Giants in the World Series, they didn't come close to filling up the park. But this summer the City of the Quakers has gone base-ball mad as four teams—Chicago, Cleveland, Detroit, and Philadelphia—have played leapfrog with first place in the hottest pennant race of the young century. Now, though, with only one week left in the regular season, two of the teams have dropped off the chase—the White Sox, the "hitless wonders" who swept last year's World Series; and the Cleveland "Naps," as they are called in tribute to their star player-manager, Napoleon Lajoie.

Last Friday, when Connie Mack's Athletics took the field be-hind their Chippewa curveballer, Chief Bender, they were one-half game in front of the Tigers, who countered with their ace, Wild Bill Donovan. Though the A's cuffed him for thirteen hits, Donovan held on for a 5–4 victory. Rain washed out Sat-urday's contest, which was rescheduled for today as the second game of a doubleheader. What about yesterday, you ask? Sun-day ball will not be legal in the state of Pennsylvania till 1934.

So it has come down to this: If the Tigers can take both ends of the twin bill, they will almost certainly capture the pennant. Even if they only get a split, they will still leave town in first place and will enjoy a scheduling edge over the A's: Detroit's last seven matches will be with the Washington Senators and St. Louis Browns, two weaklings, while the A's will have to contend with Mr. Lajoie's formidable Naps, in addition to the Senators.

The players are out on the field now, loosening up for the game. Warming up in foul territory for the A's is Jimmy Dygert, a chunky right-hander whose spitball has baffled the league this season. Do you recognize that tall, muscular guy over in left field, joking with the fans? He's Rube Waddell, the A's left-handed flamethrower, who leads the league in strikeouts every year. But don't expect to see him pitch today. He's been having a running feud with several of his teammates. Tired of Rube's antics off the field and lack of dedication on it, they have given him halfhearted support in recent outings. This bad blood may have cost the A's three or four games they ought to have won; today, Mack knows, is no time for less than all-out effort.

While we're on the subject of running feuds, look over there in the right-field corner, where young Ty Cobb is exercising by himself. Only twenty years old, he's on his way to the first of twelve batting titles, yet half the Tigers won't speak to him and several have fought him with their fists. Despite his slashing bat and his savage abandon on the base paths, young Tyrus came within a hairbreadth of being traded this spring. New manager Hughie Jennings, fed up with all the bickering on his team, arranged a deal with the New York Highlanders (later known as the Yankees) whereby Detroit would swap the greatest hitter of all time for a nondescript pitcher named Buffalo Bill Hogg. Only a last-minute hesitance kept Cobb from one day playing in the same outfield with Babe Ruth!

But enough talk of what might have been. It is nearly time to play ball. Hey, what's that commotion in the grandstand? The frustrated fans who were locked outside the park at one o'clock are now pouring over the right-field fence. The Keystone Cops rush toward the disturbance, but they don't have a chance. One gate-crasher they could nab, or ten, but not the hundreds who are scaling the wall. And look behind you—now they are cascading over the entire length of the outfield fence, thousands of them! The already crowded standing-room section begins to resemble a New York City subway car at rush hour.

As I was about to say before the ruckus started, Detroit will go with Donovan again. He's had two days' rest, all he really needs (a few weeks ago this workhorse beat Cleveland twice in two days). And besides, Philly is Bill's home town. His family

and friends are in the park, and Jennings wants to give him a chance to show off.

Donovan has been remarkable all year long. After closing the books on 1906 with a 9–15 mark, his worst ever, the thirty-year-old hurler decided he didn't want to pitch anymore; he figured he was a pretty good hitter, and declared that from now on he'd play first base. Jennings knew better than to believe him. He let Donovan play a little first base in spring camp, but held him out of action once the season began. April passed and so did much of May with Donovan on the bench, begging to return to the mound. But Ee-Yah Hughie (a nickname he earned by his blood-curdling shouts of "Ee-Yah!" to urge on his team) let Bill cool his heels on the sidelines until May 24, when he was finally permitted to pitch. His pent-up energies burst forth on the American League to the tune of 25 victories against only 4 defeats—and he might easily have gone 29–0, because his four losses came by scores of 1–0, 4–3, 4–2, and 4–1!

A roar rises from the crowd as Dygert strolls to the mound and the other A's take their positions: Ossie Schreck behind the

Gatecrashers swell Columbia Park to bursting; thousands more pay twenty-five cents a head for roof views.

plate, Home Run Harry Davis at first, Danny Murphy at second, Simon Nicholls at short, Hall-of-Famer Jimmy Collins at the hot corner; and an outfield of, left to right, Topsy Hartsel, Rube Oldring, and Socks Seybold. Defensively the A's are steady but not sensational. Except for Oldring and Nicholls, who are first-year starters, the other six fielders are "graybeards" over thirty, and three of them are on the steep part of their downhill slide—Collins, thirty-seven; Seybold, thirty-six; and Davis, thirty-four.

The avalanche of fence-vaulters continues even as Dygert sends his first pitch in to Davy Jones, Detroit's slap-hitting left-fielder. But as the Tigers go down in the first without a hit, the procession slows to a trickle and finally ends. There simply isn't a square inch of space left in which to put one more rooter.

Now the Tigers take their turn in the field. The battery is Donovan and Boss Schmidt, an ex-boxer whose fist shattered

Cobb's nose last year; the inner ring consists of Claude Rossman at first, Germany Schaefer at the second sack, Charley O'Leary at short, and Rowdy Bill Coughlin at third; the outer circle shows Jones in left and Hall-of-Famers Sam Crawford and Cobb in center and right. Both offensively and defensively, the strength of this young club—not a starter over thirty—resides in the outfield, though Rossman, too, is first-rate.

There is a buzz of anticipation in the air as Topsy Hartsel steps to the plate. And what's more, there are two brass bands, cowbells, cymbals, gongs, sirens, bugles, frying pans—all banging and clattering together to unnerve the Detroit fielders. Hartsel, a 5'5" mighty mite, is an ideal leadoff man whose specialty is drawing the base on balls and letting the heavy hitters bring him around. This time, however, Hartsel rips a Donovan fastball for a single, and on the first pitch to Nicholls, he steals second. Connie Mack has identified the weak link in the Detroit defense—catcher Schmidt's erratic arm—and has exploited it immediately. Nicholls lays down a sacrifice bunt and Hartsel takes third. It's only the first frame, but the A's are playing for one run. Clearly Mack doesn't think he'll be getting many more off Wild Bill.

Now the managerial wheels are really spinning. Jennings moves his infield in, unwilling to concede the run on a hard-hit grounder; but Donovan spoils the strategy by walking Seybold. Now the shortstop and second baseman must pull back for a possible double-play ball. And Harry Davis complies, smacking one to the shortstop's left—but the ball kicks off O'Leary to second-baseman Schaefer, who picks it up and throws . . . too late. It's a hit. The run is in, Athletics occupy first and second, and there is still only one man down.

Danny Murphy follows with a bunt toward first which he beats out, loading the bases. Donovan has not exactly been bludgeoned, but he is being nibbled to death. Jimmy Collins lifts a fly to left, deep enough to score Seybold. Two down, but the A's will not let go of the Tiger tail yet. Oldring wallops a ball into the overflow crowd here in center field, a ground-rule double, and Davis comes home to make the count 3–0. The fans are giving a razzing to Donovan now, and his partisans, seated in the third-base deck, look awfully glum. At last Schreck is retired, and the A's take the field to an ovation.

Claude Rossman opens the Tiger second with a single to center. Coughlin then raps one to the mound but Dygert, in his haste to start the double play in motion, throws the ball into the dirt and both men are safe. Here's Schmidt, brandishing his big war club as he steps into the batter's box. He squares to bunt, and delicately lays one down to advance the runners. Just between you and me, I think Schmidt ought to have swung away. With the eighth- and ninth-place hitters to follow, and his team down 3–0, this was no time for Jennings to give up an out. Yes, second-guessing the manager is a bit unfair, but who can resist?

O'Leary, a little fellow with a very light stick, also knocks one back to Dygert, who once again sets his sights on Rossman, now hung up between third and home. Back and forth Claude dances, trying to give O'Leary time to reach second base. Back and forth, back and forth in the rundown—until Dygert fires one to Schreck at close range that bounces off his chest protector. Rossman rushes past him to score. 3–1. Now Dygert's errant tosses in the field take their effect on the mound. He sends four wide ones to Donovan, loading the bases. Mr. Mack invites the rattled youngster to soothe his nerves with an early shower and in comes—Rube Waddell!

Connie Mack is a hunch player, and he's playing a big one now: First of all, that Waddell woke up sober this morning, and second, that his teammates would not throw away a pennant just to deny the Rube a win. As it turns out, Rube does not put his fielders to the test. Coming in with the bases loaded, he fans Davy Jones and Germany Schaefer with a combination of rising fastballs and explosive curves, then struts around the mound as the fans go wild. In later years Branch Rickey is to say that "when Waddell had control—and some sleep—he was unbeatable." Rube must have had a very tranquil Sunday night, for he fans Cobb and Rossman in the third and Schmidt and O'Leary in the fourth, making it six strikeout victims of the eight men he's faced.

While Waddell is making tabby cats of the Bengals, the A's resume their assault on Donovan. Socks Seybold opens the third with a double to right and chugs home on Davis's two-bagger to left. Murphy's bunt single then advances Davis to third, from where he scores on Oldring's force-out.

The 5–1 lead looks like money in the bank, and the A's even widen their margin in the fifth. Home Run Harry Davis, the league's four-base champ the last three years, leads off with his specialty, a booming drive over the scoreboard in right. Murphy is put down, but Jimmy Collins drives one against the scoreboard and into the crowd for an automatic double. Umpire Silk O'Loughlin jogs out to request return of the ball, as is the custom of the times, and the gentleman in the bowler hat who caught it assents.

Jennings has still given no sign to his bullpen—either he doesn't wish to embarrass Wild Bill in front of his folks; or he has given up on the contest and, with another game yet to play today, doesn't want to deplete his small staff. Whichever is the case, the A's are pleased to continue the shellacking. Oldring whacks a drive toward the corner in left. Davy Jones drifts back on the ball until he senses the crowd behind him, then, as is his habit, shies off; the catchable ball drops into the first row of standees for a run-scoring double.

The fifth inning ends without further ado as Donovan whiffs Schreck and Waddell. Loping toward the bench, Jones is intercepted at third base by a bunch of angry teammates; they

Rube Waddell can be awesome when he has a mind to be—the 349 men he fanned in 1904 will not be topped until 1965.

threaten him with all sorts of mayhem if the game is lost, as now seems certain. Davy's faintheartedness has cost his team a run; however, one run doesn't look so very large when you're trailing 7–1.

But the complexion of the game changes radically in the top of the seventh, as shabby Philadelphia fielding enables the Tigers to tally four times on only one hit. Oldring muffs Donovan's lazy fly to open the door, and then Waddell experiences his first lapse of control, walking Jones. Schaefer follows with a perfect double-play grounder to Nicholls, but the kid kicks it.

Now the bases are loaded for Sam Crawford, the left-handed slugger who played alongside Waddell in the old Western League in 1899 and who, like the Rube, will be honored with a plaque in Cooperstown. So far today, Crawford has had no luck with Waddell; but this time Rube gets a pitch up in the strike zone where Sam likes it, and the ball goes sailing over Seybold's head for two bases and two runs.

Cobb, up next, has gone out weakly in his previous trips to the plate and does so once more; but Schaefer scores as Ty is thrown out at first. Crawford, who advanced to third on the play, himself comes in to score as Murphy scoops up Rossman's ground shot in the hole and fires to first in time. Coughlin, too, is put out, but the Tigers are now in striking distance at 7–5.

The A's get one back in their half of the inning on a single by Murphy, sacrifice by Collins, single by Oldring, and ground-out by Schreck. Staggering through seven innings, Donovan has been walloped for fourteen hits, but Jennings will not take him out unless he asks out. And Wild Bill won't ask.

Fred Payne, who replaced Boss Schmidt behind the plate a few innings back, is retired to lead off the eighth. But O'Leary doubles and daringly steals third with Donovan at the bat. Wild Bill cannot bring him home, but Davy Jones does, with a single that cancels out the run he gave the A's in the fifth inning.

Well, here we are in the top of the ninth with the A's still up by a score of 8–6. Waddell has shown signs of weakening, but Mack will stick with him as the left-handed heart of the Tiger batting order—Crawford, Cobb, and Rossman—comes up. (In 1907 there are not yet any relief specialists on the lines of a Bruce Sutter or Rich Gossage; and with pitching staffs that comprise five or at most six men, managers cannot play Captain Hook, yanking hurlers as they please.)

When Crawford loops a single over second base, the boisterous crowd falls into a moment's eerie silence—but erupts again as Cobb stands in for his turn. The Georgia Peach stirs up silent admiration for his skills and vocal hostility for his attacking, almost driven style of play. In a series with the Highlanders earlier this month he scored from first base on Rossman's sacrifice bunt! Like a man possessed, he circled the bases at full tilt while the stunned New Yorkers fumbled the ball around. Cobb doesn't play just to beat you; he wants to destroy you, and the A's rooters have taken particular delight in his futility at the plate today.

Waddell starts Cobb off with a fastball up and in, a tough pitch for Ty, who leans over the plate. He nonchalantly watches it go by. Waddell figures Cobb is looking for a ball out over the plate, perhaps one he can punch to the opposite field. So, Rube will say in later years, "I throws another for the inside corner and the second the ball leaves my hand I know I made a bum guess. This Cobb, who didn't seem to notice the first one, steps back like he had the catcher's sign, takes a toehold, and swings. I guess the ball's goin' yet."

Out it soars, over the right fielder, over the roped-in fans, and over the fence, coming to earth in the middle of 29th Street. A tie game! Connie Mack is so stunned he falls off the end of the A's bench, landing on a pile of bats. Cobb is not a home-run hitter—no one really is in this decade, not even Home Run

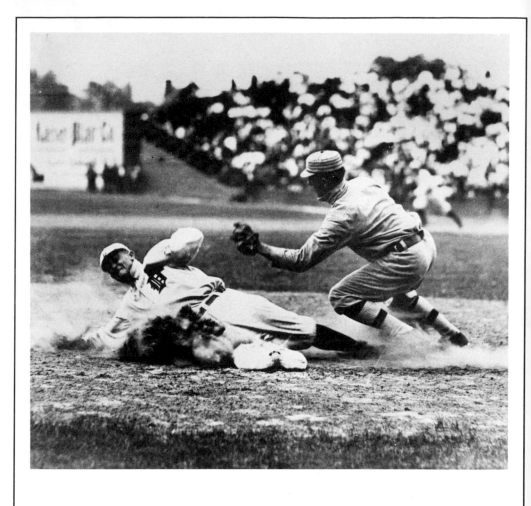

No one has ever run the bases so daringly as Ty Cobb. Thirty-five times he stole home plate, and three times he stole second, third, and home in the same inning.

Harry Davis, who will top the league with eight. And besides, the ball Cobb hit had been in play since the fifth inning and must have been pretty beat up. How could he have sent it so far? And did he steal the sign as Waddell suspected?

How he managed to wallop it so far no one can explain, but Cobb did know that he would get another fastball up and in. By casually letting the first pitch go by, he duped Waddell into thinking he was looking for a pitch away. Ty figured that Rube would try to cross him up and fire another in the identical spot. He was so confident he had pegged Rube's thoughts that as Waddell uncorked the pitch he jumped back off the plate and swung with everything he had in him.

Mack, scrambling to his feet, waves his scorecard frantically toward the bullpen. The great Eddie Plank, whom Mack had intended to hold out for the second game, comes running in as Waddell trudges slowly to the clubhouse. Mack's gamble on the Rube has proved a bust. Plank tosses in a few warm-up throws to Mike Powers, who has replaced Schreck, then sets down Rossman, Coughlin, and Payne in order.

Donovan blanks Philly in the ninth and tenth, and in the eleventh takes the mound to defend a lead. In the top of the inning Cobb had hit another long drive to right, this one landing in the overflow crowd, and Rossman had followed with a single to put Detroit up 9–8. But in the A's half, Nicholls doubles, Wild Bill wild-pitches him to third, and the run comes in on Davis's long fly.

The Tigers threaten in the twelfth, loading the bases with two outs, but Hartsel catches up with Crawford's drive down the left-field line. The A's also fail to score.

This game is nearly three hours old, a common enough duration today but quite uncommon at the turn of the century, when games were usually completed in ninety minutes or less. If someone doesn't win pretty soon, there won't be enough daylight to play the second game. With each passing moment, victory becomes more and more urgent for the A's. If the second game is not played today, no makeup will be scheduled.

Donovan and Plank breeze through the thirteenth. Though he must be weary from all the pitches he's thrown, Wild Bill is getting better as the contest wears on. In the early part of the game he seemed to have been throwing his "drop ball" (or sinker, as we know it) too hard, not giving it a chance to rotate and dip. Coming in straight as a string, it proved very hittable. But now as he tires, his arm-swing slows and he gets more "action" on the ball.

In the bottom of the fourteenth, Bill serves up a fastball to Harry Davis that the powerful first-sacker drives to deep center. Here comes Crawford racing back to the rope · · · he is leaning against the crowd to brace for the catch. But now a policeman runs in front of him, obscuring Sam's view with that comical high bobby's hat. The ball lands at Crawford's feet and bounds into the crowd!

Davis is perched at second base, believing he's hit a ground-rule double. But Jones and Cobb are racing out to center field to confront umpire O'Loughlin; they and Crawford believe interference should be called and the batter ruled out. The stadium is in an uproar. O'Loughlin, whose call it properly is, wavers and wavers, infuriating both the Tigers and the A's. At last he decides there *was* interference, and calls Davis out. But Silk's colleague, Tommy Connolly, who was behind the plate (only two umps work a game at this time), now offers *his* opinion— namely, that there was no interference and Davis should hold second base. Back and forth the players race between the umpires as the dispute rages. Even Connie Mack, known as a mild-mannered man for all his sixty-six years in baseball, uncharacteristically leaves the bench and harangues O'Loughlin long and loud.

Utter pandemonium erupts. The A's clear their bench and

come galloping out to center field, followed in no time by the entire Tiger team. Nearly a thousand fans join them on the outfield grass, as do the police. Monte Cross, a fifteen-year veteran closing out his career as the A's backup shortstop, rushes into the mob with his fists doubled. He is promptly decked by Charley O'Leary. Cross then dusts himself off and sets upon Claude Rossman, who gives back what he got and more. As Cross is being pummeled, to the rescue comes Waddell, freshly showered and in street clothes. Donovan grabs Waddell and tries to restrain him, but Rube will not be denied his fun, and tears loose. Donovan, however, is arrested by a cop who sees a chance to serve his home town as never before.

Now Germany Schaefer approaches the policeman and sweetly points out to him, "My good man, you can't arrest Donovan. Why, the stands are filled with his Irish relatives. Pinch him, and they'll tear us apart."

"Perhaps I acted hastily," the cop concedes, releasing Donovan and collaring Rossman.

At last the warring factions are untangled and Rossman, too, is released. Seeking to reestablish their authority, the umpires declare Davis out because of the policeman's interference; they also banish both Rossman and Cross. Pitcher Ed Killian is recruited to replace Rossman at first base, and play resumes. The fans, who have slowly subsided in their anger, flare up anew as Danny Murphy singles. They know full well that Davis would have come in with the winning run on that hit.

As the autumn sky dims, the game winds on. It is plain now that there will be no second contest, and that the A's must win this one to regain first place. But they are unable to mount another threat; that wild fourteenth inning seems to have done them in. Plank continues to pitch masterfully; though he allows Cobb to reach third in the top of the seventeenth, he strands him there.

Bill Donovan

In the home half, young Eddie Collins pinch-hits for Oldring and singles, but does not score either. With the players scarcely able to see the ball and, by Cobb's description, "guess-hitting," at ten minutes to six the umpires call the game. It goes down in the record books as a tie.

But in fact the Tigers are the winners, for they retain their hold on first place. They go on to Washington, where in the opener they will come from behind to defeat a raw-boned rookie named Walter Johnson. While Detroit is sweeping the four-game set with the Senators, the A's will drop one to the Naps. Despite the final-week heroics of Jimmy Dygert, who will hurl three shutouts in four days, the Mackmen are dead.

Who were the heroes of this remarkable game? Cobb, certainly; his homer—one of only eleven the Tigers hit *all season long*—kept the game alive in the ninth and provided him with what he would always call his greatest day. For the A's, old Harry Davis, who drove in four runs, and young Rube Oldring, who drove in three. And Rube Waddell, who deserved a better fate.

And most of all, Bill Donovan, who allowed eight runs and fourteen hits through seven innings, and only one run and six hits over the next ten. Wild Bill threw well over two hundred pitches for the game in a display of stamina and heart the likes of which we will surely not see again.

DETROIT	AB	R	H	P	A	E
Jones, lf.	7	1	1	5	0	0
Schaefer, 2b.	9	1	3	3	6	0
Crawford, cf.-1b. ..	8	2	2	7	0	0
Cobb, rf.	8	2	3	1	0	0
Rossman, 1b.	7	1	2	13	2	0
Killian, 1b.	0	0	0	1	0	0
Mullin, 1b.	1	0	0	0	0	0
Downs, cf.	1	0	0	2	0	0
Coughlin, 3b.	7	0	0	1	3	0
Schmidt, c.	1	0	0	3	1	1
Payne, c.	6	0	1	9	1	0
O'Leary, ss.	8	1	2	3	1	0
Donovan, p.	7	1	1	3	7	0
TOTALS	70	9	15	51	21	1

PHILADELPHIA	AB	R	H	P	A	E
Hartsel, lf.	9	1	4	3	0	0
Nicholls, ss.	6	1	2	4	9	1
Seybold, rf.	6	2	1	1	0	0
*Davis, 1b.	8	3	3	19	1	0
Murphy, 2b.	7	1	4	2	6	0
*J. Collins, 3b. ...	8	1	1	3	3	0
Oldring, cf.	7	0	3	3	0	1
a E. Collins	1	0	1	0	0	0
Schreck, c.	3	0	0	9	1	1
Powers, c.	4	0	0	4	0	1
Dygert, p.	0	0	0	0	0	2
Waddell, p.	4	0	0	1	0	0
Plank, p.	4	0	1	2	1	0
TOTALS	67	9	20	51	21	6

a Singled for Oldring in 17th
* Charged with AB for Sac. Fly, in accordance with scoring rules of 1907

```
DETROIT        010  000  412  010  000  00 — 9
PHILADELPHIA   302  020  100  010  000  00 — 9
```

RBI—Crawford 2, Cobb 3, Rossman 2, Jones, Davis 4, Oldring 3, J. Collins, Schreck. 2B—Hartsel 3, Nicholls, Davis, Oldring 2, J. Collins, Crawford, Cobb, O'Leary. HR—Davis, Cobb. SB—Coughlin, O'Leary, Cobb, Hartsel. Sac.—Schmidt, Crawford, Nicholls 2, J. Collins, Powers. LOB—Det. 17, Phi. 13. Umpires—O'Loughlin, Connolly. Time—3:50. Att.—24,127.

DETROIT	IP	H	R	ER	BB	SO
Donovan	17	20	9	9	3	11

PHILADELPHIA	IP	H	R	ER	BB	SO
Dygert	1⅓	1	1	0	1	0
**Waddell	6⅔	7	7	3	1	7
Plank	9	7	1	1	2	3

**Pitched to two batters in 9th
HBP—Plank (1). WP—Donovan (1)

May 2, 1917
Cincinnati Reds
vs.
Chicago Cubs

Baseball has a long season. Although it's thought of as the summer game, play begins in the rawness of spring and ends in the chill of autumn, with the games played in between serving mostly to set up the drama of September and the spectacle of October. We just witnessed two top-notch teams playing their hearts out before a packed stadium, knowing that a championship hung in the balance, and that's the way it will be with most of the games we will go on to attend together. But the great majority of games do not, in the way that a World Series game does, give advance notice of their potential for greatness. It is one of these unpromising games we will see this afternoon. Two mediocre teams, playing on the worst field in the big leagues under weather conditions that would make Bowie Kuhn blush, are about to present the greatest game ever pitched.

The teams are the Cincinnati Reds and the Chicago Cubs, destined for fourth and fifth place, respectively. The place is Chicago's Weeghman Park, constructed in 1914 for the Chicago Whales of the Federal League, that short-lived attempt to establish a third major league. When the outlaw circuit folded last year, Whales' owner Charles Weeghman, whose fortune was built on Weeghman's Cafés, a Chicago lunchroom chain, was permitted to buy the Cubs. He immediately endeared himself to the fans by proclaiming a policy, new to baseball, of permitting them to keep any ball hit into the stands, and by transferring the Cubs from their crumbling West Side Park to his spanking-new and vacant edifice.

In later years this smallish park, which seats only 14,000, will be expanded to become Wrigley Field. But on this day Weeghman Park has no need for extra seats—only 2,500 curious souls have come out to see how baseball can be played in a 38-degree chill, which because of high winds gusting off Lake Michigan feels colder still. What's more, the arctic conditions have caused the topsoil dumped on this cow pasture of a playing field to crack and shift. Seeing the infielders wrestle with ground balls on this grassless, "skin" diamond should prove amusing; and since there is an uneven slope between the infield and the outfield, even routine pop flies beyond the infield will carry an element of risk.

With the park only one-fifth filled, the ushers will look the other way; we can take whichever seats we like. A box along the third-base line, you say? A good choice—let's take our places, throw a blanket over our legs, and have a look at the Cubs while they attempt to warm up. Nearest to us at third base is Charlie Deal, a twenty-five-year-old for whom the Cubs are his fifth big-league team. If he learns to hit even a little bit, he can unpack his bags, for he has a fine glove. The shortstop is Rollie Zeider, a thirty-four-year-old utility man who has played every position but catcher and pitcher during his career, and has played none particularly well. Like Deal, he carries a light stick. The second baseman is new to the Cubs this year: "Laughing Larry" Doyle, who ten years ago uttered the oft-quoted line "It's great to be young and a Giant." No longer young and no longer a Giant, this veteran has starred for the Cubs at the bat in the early going; however, he was never a great second baseman, and his range is diminishing season by season.

At first is Fred Merkle, who like Doyle was a long-time Giant; the Cubs acquired him from Brooklyn in the first week of this season. Fred is a pretty fair all-around player who will never live down the infamy of his "boner," which cost the Giants the 1908 pennant. On September 23 of that year, with two outs in the ninth inning of a tie game with the Cubs, Merkle was on first when a base hit scored the "winning" run from third. Merkle, as was the custom of the day, did not bother to touch second base. The Cubs, on an appeal play, claimed a force-out at second which nullified the run. The umpires upheld the appeal, but since the New York fans had spilled onto the field, play could not be resumed and the game was declared a tie. When the season itself ended in a tie between the Giants and Cubs, a replay of "the Merkle Game" was necessitated, and the Cubs won it.

Out in left is Les Mann, a dependable .270 hitter and good flyhawk who, like Deal, Zeider, and catcher Art Wilson, is a former Federal Leaguer. In center is slugger Cy Williams, who last year led the league in home runs with 12. He came to the Cubs straight from the Notre Dame campus back in 1912, and will still be playing major-league ball in 1930. The right fielder is Harry Wolter, a seven-year major-league vet whom the

Throughout his career, Jim "Hippo" Vaughn has been a very good pitcher with some very bad ball clubs (the 1917 Cubs are no exception). With better support, he might have amassed Hall-of-Fame credentials.

Yankees sent to the minors in 1913, where he stayed until the Cubs rescued him this year. Harry will hit .249 in 1917, then drift back down for good. And the catcher is Art Wilson, another Giant castoff who joined the Cubbies last year. Though squat and strong at 5'8" and 170 pounds, Art is a weak hitter who is prized for his work behind the plate.

Obviously, the eight Cubs in the field are not an impressive crew. But on the mound, that's another story. Jim "Hippo" Vaughn is a fireballing left-hander whose nickname derives less from his size—6'4", 220 pounds—than from his lumbering gait. In the last three years he has won 57 games with little support, and in the next four he will win 85 more. When this season is over, his record will read 23 wins, 13 losses, and an ERA of 2.01. He has been particularly tough on the Reds, whom he defeated in Cincinnati last week, fanning eleven.

The Cubs finished as high as fifth last year only because of their mound staff; as a team they hit .239, second poorest in the league. This year, with the addition of such new faces as Merkle, Doyle, Deal, Wolter, and Wilson, plus a new manager in Fred Mitchell, the Chicagoans are challenging for the lead on the strength of their improved batting. Yesterday they scored seven runs in the seventh to beat the Cards, 9–0; in the next two days they will blast the Reds by 10–3 and 11–2. But their bats will cool as the weather warms, and the "new-look" Cubs will finish in fifth place once again, with a team batting average of— you guessed it—.239.

Heinie Groh, the man due to lead off for the Reds against Vaughn, takes off his heavy, shawl-collar sweater (they won't wear jackets till the twenties) and strolls to the plate, lugging the oddest bat you'll ever see. Heinie (real name: Henry) calls it his "bottle bat" because of its enormous barrel and long, skinny handle. Though the bat weighs forty-six ounces, far more than any bat used in the majors in the 1980s, almost all the weight is in the untapered barrel. This bat enables Heinie to choke up, yet still get good wood on the ball even if he's jammed in on the hands.

Vaughn has trouble gripping the ball in this murderous cold, missing the plate by wide margins with his first two pitches. Nonetheless, he comes back to fan Groh. Switch-hitter Larry Kopf, the next batter, taps a soft grounder to Doyle for out number two. Next is Greasy Neale, another switch-hitter, who is on his way to a .294 season, the finest of his life; in later years he will win greater fame as a football coach. He swings at the first pitch, a fastball, and lifts a pop in back of second base. Williams, playing a shallow center field, races in, calls Doyle off the play, and makes the catch to end the inning.

Now the Reds rush out into the field, the steam of their escaping breath showing clearly in the frigid air. Like the Cubs, the Reds had half a ball club last year—their batters were second best in the league, and their hurlers were second worst. This year, under the expert tutelage of new manager Christy Mathewson—the former great hurler of the Giants—the pitching will improve markedly, and the Reds will rise from seventh to fourth.

At third is Heinie Groh, the best at his position in the National League. Only 5′8″ and 158 pounds, Heinie packs a surprising wallop with his bottle bat—he doesn't hit home runs, but this year he will lead NL batters with 39 doubles. At short is Larry Kopf, a pesky hitter and ever-improving fielder. Though he still commits more errors than he should, he also reaches more balls than most shortstops. Second base is an annual problem for Cincinnati: in the six-year span of 1914–19, each spring will produce a new man at the keystone. This year's walk-on is Davey Shean, a thirty-eight-year-old "brainy" veteran who can't hit a lick; he drifted out of the majors back in 1912 and has been resuscitated by the Reds out of desperation. At first is the thirty-four-year-old Hal Chase, last year's bat champ, who can play first base better than anyone has before or since. However, "Prince Hal," as he is called for his haughty manner as well as for his peerless play at first, is subject to streaks of inept play at the worst possible moments. Next year Mathewson will charge him with betting against his own team and kicking routine plays in order to cash in his bets; and after the following season Chase will leave the majors under a cloud, known to be one of the figures involved in fixing the 1919 World Series.

In left field is Manny Cueto, a 5'5" Havana stogie who also plays three infield positions and occasionally catches. His versatility does not extend to the batter's box, where he frightens no pitcher. He is playing today because Neale, the regular left fielder, has moved over to center to fill in for Edd Roush, a future Hall-of-Famer who is out with a bum leg. Around in right is one of the great figures in American sport, Jim Thorpe. Unfortunately, the Oklahoma Sac and Fox Indian plays every other sport better than he does baseball. An Olympic hero in 1912, he was forced to return his decathlon and pentathlon medals when it was revealed he had accepted money to play in a summer baseball league in 1909. A few days after this disqualification, he signed a multiyear contract with the Giants in a publicity stunt. He can run like the wind and throw like a cannon, but he cannot hit a curveball.

The catcher is Hap Huhn, a seldom-used reserve whose right-handed bat puts him in the all-right-handed lineup against Vaughn. On the mound is Cincinnati's best, Fred Toney. After a spectacular performance in minor-league ball when he threw a *seventeen-inning* no-hitter, striking out nineteen, Toney came up with the team he faces today. But the big right-hander—if Vaughn is called Hippo, Toney may be called a whale—was bothered by Chicago manager Johnny Evers's browbeating style, and did not stick. This year, under Mathewson's easygoing directorship, Toney will flourish, going on to record 24 wins. He throws a variety of stuff: spitballs, fastballs, curves, and an overhand sinker that fades away from left-handed batters just as Christy Mathewson's "fadeaway," or screwball, did just a few years ago.

Fred sets Zeider, Wolter, and Doyle down in order in the first, but two balls are smacked with authority. The cold is troubling Toney more than it did Vaughn, and it will be some time until he begins to feel right.

Vaughn easily retires Chase, Thorpe, and Shean on infield outs in the top of the second; but Toney's struggle to find his stuff continues. He tries a spitball against leadoff batter Merkle but the ball, instead of dropping like a stone as it reaches the plate, hangs belt-high, big as a grapefruit. Merkle whacks it, but right at Groh, who is nearly carried into left field by the force of the drive. Next is Cy Williams, who has "owned" Toney in the past. Pitching cautiously, Fred walks him. Manager Mitchell signals a hit-and-run play, and with Williams on the go, Mann grounds to Groh. Heinie makes the play across the diamond as Williams crosses to second. There he dies, as Wilson pops out to Kopf.

In the Reds' third, Cueto skies to second, Huhn rolls out to Vaughn, and Toney fans. If the cold is tough on the pitchers, it is no picnic for the batters either. That horsehide-covered ball of yarn comes in there like a mortar shell, and the unlucky man who hits one off the handle will feel the vibrations for half an inning.

Toney now disposes of the Cubs more easily than he did in his first two frames: Deal grounds out to Groh, Vaughn taps one to Chase at first, and Zeider pops to Chase in short right field. Not much excitement yet; but that's the way it is with pitching duels until the late innings, when what each batter does stands

*Fred Toney is on his way to a great season; six weeks from now he
will win both ends of a doubleheader, allowing a total of six hits.*

out clearly. In the early going, a procession of thwarted bats-men can make your mind wander to, say, someplace where it's *warm*. At least these old-time pitchers don't dawdle on the mound.

In the Reds' fourth, Groh extracts a walk from Vaughn (he's one of the best in the game at this). Now Kopf slaps the ball to Doyle, who feints at the oncoming Groh and stops him dead in his tracks, then flips to first to retire Kopf. Merkle immediately fires on to Zeider, who makes the tag on the sliding Groh, and the Cubs have a double play. Neale follows with a bouncer to Zeider, who boots it. On the first pitch to Chase, Neale takes off for second on a steal attempt. Wilson rifles the ball to Doyle covering, and the side is retired.

Courtesy of Cincinnati's poor baserunning, Vaughn has passed through the first four frames facing the minimum twelve batters. But Toney keeps pace, getting Wolter on a pop to Shean; Doyle on a fly to Cueto at the foul line; and Merkle on a pop to Groh.

Vaughn strikes out the side in the fifth, but receives his first scare as Thorpe's blistering liner to left lands foul by less than a foot. In the bottom of the inning, Toney is again wary of Wil-liams and walks him. Mann follows with a line drive to Cueto for the first out. When Wilson sends a looper to second, Shean decides to allow the ball to drop at his feet, hoping for the twin killing. And it almost works: Williams is only twenty feet from first base, awaiting the catch to return to first base; Shean picks the ball up on the bounce and fires to Chase for the tag on Wil-liams, but Prince Hal cannot beat Wilson to first, so the result of the trickery is simply a force-out. With two Cubs down, Deal belts a long fly to center field, where Neale makes a fine running catch.

Both sides go down quietly in the sixth. Two-thirds of the game have been completed and neither side has a base hit. If this game were being played fifty or sixty years later, everyone in the park would realize that something unusual was going on. But in 1917 a six-inning no-hitter, though it is hardly a common event, does not arouse much notice among the fans. As for the players, they are focused on the 0–0 score and grow increasingly tense as it becomes increasingly certain that the first team to score will win the game.

Groh leads off the seventh by taking the first pitch, a fast-ball, for a ball. Vaughn has established a pattern of throwing a fastball on the first pitch, and usually throwing it for a strike. Now he comes back with a curve, which Groh also takes, thinking it to be outside; but umpire Al Orth calls it good. Groh grumbles a bit, but when the next pitch is another curve in the same spot, and Orth calls "Strike Two," Groh really laces into him, maligning his eyesight, his impartiality (Orth and Vaughn were teammates long ago), and the circumstances of his birth. The man in blue lets Groh go on for a while; but when he refuses to step back in the batter's box, up goes the thumb and out goes Groh. Mathewson sends up spare infielder Gus Getz to complete the time at bat; he will take Groh's place at third in the bottom of the inning. Vaughn may have been thrown off his stride by the fuss at home plate, for he gives Getz a walk. But Kopf once again supplies a double play, this time of a more conventional variety: Vaughn fields Kopf's tap to the box, whirls, and fires to Doyle, who relays the ball on to Merkle. Neale pops to Wilson, and the "threat" is over.

Although the weather has not improved a whit since the game began—if anything, the temperature has dropped a degree or two—Toney seems to be throwing more loosely in the bottom of the seventh. He gets Doyle and Merkle on a pop foul and a grounder, and his nemesis, Cy Williams, on a pop to Shean.

Vaughn blazes by the Reds in the eighth, whiffing both Thorpe and Shean for the second time. Then, sitting in the dugout while his mates take their swings in the bottom of the frame, Hippo hears a yell at the far end of the Cub bench: "Come on, let's get a run off this guy!"

"Run, heck; we haven't even got a hit off him!" comes the retort.

"Well," observes another, "they haven't got one off Hippo either."

Only now does Vaughn realize that he is pitching a no-hitter. Out on the mound, Toney does not know it yet; he, too, will catch on when his team comes in to bat. He gets Mann and Deal on outfield flies, and Wilson on a dribbler to short.

Eight innings are complete, farther than any two teams have come without a base hit to show between them. Which pitcher will be the first to crack? Surely one of them must, for while the odds against either pitcher's hurling a no-hitter are approximately five hundred to one, the odds against both pitchers' accomplishing the feat are more than two hundred fifty thousand to one!

Vaughn comes out for the ninth determined not to risk blowing the no-hitter by hanging a curve, particularly since the bottom of the Reds' order is due up. They will see nothing but fastballs. He gets a scare as the first batter, Manny Cueto, lines the ball hard, but right at Deal, who doesn't have to move a step. Then Hippo takes matters in his own hands, striking out Hap Huhn and, on three straight blazers, Toney as well. He has his no-hitter, and what a no-hitter it is, too. Facing the minimum twenty-seven batters, he has struck out ten and has allowed only one ball out of the infield—and that, back in the first inning, might easily have been caught by the second baseman. Vaughn has been magnificent, but the Cubs still must push a run across.

As Toney takes the mound for the bottom of the ninth, the air is frozen with tension. A few fans rouse themselves from the cold to broadcast a shout of encouragement to the Cub batters, but they are howling into the wind. Toney will not be denied. He nails Vaughn on a weak pop to Getz, Zeider on a routine grounder to Getz, and Wolter on a pop-up, also to third-base-man Getz.   Cheers for both pitchers begin to arise from the spectators, who are rabidly partisan but aware that they have been privileged to witness a double no-hitter, a feat which has never before been accomplished at any level of professional ball. If you can place your trust in the odds, baseball may produce another one sometime between the years 2050 and 2200.

But this ball game is not over, you know. Vaughn's first opponent in the tenth is Gus Getz. He sends a pop straight up the chute in front of home, which Wilson grabs easily. The next batter is Kopf, who in three trips to the plate has hit into two twin killings and grounded out. Vaughn runs the count to three and two, then fires in his old reliable, the fastball. But this time Kopf connects, driving the pitch on a line between Doyle and Merkle, who dives for the ball but misses by a foot or so. It is a single. The magic spell is over; looking at Vaughn you can see him sag with dejection, and perhaps a measure of relief. Will we now see an avalanche of hits? Neale lifts the ball to center, where Williams settles under it for out number two. Hal Chase follows with another liner to center, hit hard but well within Williams's range. The inning appears to be over as Cy moves in a step and braces for the catch. Had he moved in two or three steps, he could have made the grab at his belt buckle; as it is, the ball sinks to a level below his knees, and though he gets both hands on the ball—he muffs it. Kopf reaches third as Chase holds at first on the error.

The batter now is Thorpe, twice a strikeout victim. On Vaughn's first pitch, Chase dashes for second and steals it without a throw—Wilson holds on to the ball for fear that Kopf will

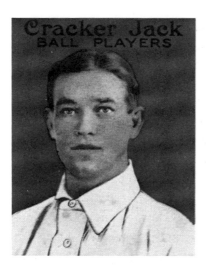

Hal Chase

come in to score while the play is being executed at second. Vaughn now goes to the curveball; Thorpe, struggling to hold his weight back on the pitch, swings awkwardly and hits it right off the hands. The ball bounds in front of the plate, then dribbles up the third-base line. Kopf races toward the plate with the tie-breaking run. Vaughn hurries over to make the play, knowing his third baseman can never reach it in time. He also knows he has no hope of catching the fleet-footed Thorpe at first and, in a clever bit of improvisation, shovels the ball home. When Kopf, who is right behind Vaughn—so close that were Hippo to turn around, he could tag him—sees this, he stops dead in his tracks.

But look—catcher Art Wilson is not prepared for the throw! He just stands at home plate, arms to his sides, as Vaughn's toss comes to him. The ball strikes his chest protector and drops to the ground, while Wilson fails even to make the instinctive move to grab the ball once it hits him. The stress of the game and the demands on him at this moment have caused him to blank out, to be paralyzed with indecision. Kopf, seeing Wilson standing there like a zombie as the ball rolls a few steps away, dashes home with the run. The stadium is in an uproar—the 2,500 fans sound like 25,000 as they yell for Wilson to wake up.

Vaughn looks over his shoulder and sees Chase—he has rounded third and is heading for home! Hippo turns back to

Wilson and shouts, "Are you going to let *him* score, too?" At this remark, Wilson snaps out of the deep freeze, grabs the ball, and tags the sliding Chase to end the Reds' half of the inning.

Fortified by the one-run lead, Toney opens his end of the tenth by fanning Doyle, only his second strikeout of the game. The next batter is Merkle, the only Cub who has come close to a hit, with his liner to Groh in the second. Now Fred finds another pitch to his liking and wallops it to deepest left field. Cueto goes back on the ball,

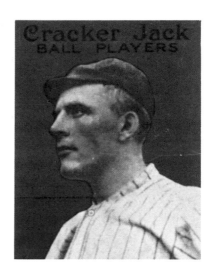

Art Wilson

back, back, leans against the wall, raises his glove, and snares the drive. But this is not the Cubs' last gasp. Toney must now get by the dangerous Williams if no-hit glory is to be his. Still cautious, Fred goes behind 2–0 on the count. Determined not to give Cy a fat pitch, he aims his next delivery high and inside; but it comes in over the heart of the plate where the lefthanded slugger can rip at it. He tomahawks a low screamer to deep right. Thorpe sprints to the line, dives, but cannot reach the ball. Fortunately for Toney, it caroms off the grandstand foul, by inches. Thorpe picks himself up, picks the ball up, and tosses it in to Shean, who relays it to Toney without inspection from umpires Orth or Rigler. When Toney looks at the ball in his glove, his eyes light up—there is a scuff the size of a silver dollar! No need to fool with breaking pitches now—just bust the ball in hard and let the air currents act on that scuff. Fred misses the corner to go 3–1 on the count, then flings the next two pitches past the baffled Williams, and this unbelievable game is over. In the Cubs' clubhouse afterwards, owner Charles Weeghman will stick his head in the door and curse his players. Art Wilson will sob like a baby and apologize to Vaughn, "I just went out on you, Jim—I just went tight." And Jim will say to a reporter, "It's just another ballgame, just another loss."

But it wasn't.

May 2, 1917

CINCINNATI

	AB	R	H	P	A	E
Groh, 3b.	1	0	0	2	3	0
a Getz	1	0	0	2	1	0
Kopf, ss.	4	1	1	1	4	0
Neale, cf.	4	0	0	1	0	0
Chase, 1b.	4	0	0	12	0	0
Thorpe, rf.	4	0	1	1	0	0
Shean, 2b.	3	0	0	3	1	0
Cueto, lf.	3	0	0	5	0	0
Huhn, c.	3	0	0	3	0	0
Toney, p.	3	0	0	0	1	0
TOTALS	30	1	2	30	10	0

CHICAGO

	AB	R	H	P	A	E
Zeider, ss.	4	0	0	1	0	1
Wolter, rf.	4	0	0	0	0	0
Doyle, 2b.	4	0	0	4	4	0
Merkle, 1b.	4	0	0	7	1	0
Williams, cf.	2	0	0	2	0	1
Mann, lf.	3	0	0	0	0	0
Wilson, c.	3	0	0	14	1	0
Deal, 3b.	3	0	0	2	0	0
Vaughn, p.	3	0	0	0	3	0
TOTALS	30	0	0	30	9	2

a Walked for Groh in 7th

```
CINCINNATI    000  000  000  1 — 1
CHICAGO       000  000  000  0 — 0
```

RBI—Thorpe. SB—Chase. CS—Neale. DP—Chi. 2. LOB—Chi. 2, Cin. 1. Umpires—Orth, Rigler. Time—1:50. Att.—2,500 (approx.).

CINCINNATI	IP	H	R	ER	BB	SO
Toney	10	0	0	0	2	3

CHICAGO						
Vaughn	10	2	1	0	2	10

October 10, 1924
New York Giants
vs.
Washington Senators

"First in war, first in peace, and last in the American League."
For nearly a quarter of a century, that description of Washington had been pretty close to the truth. But no longer. At the end of the 1924 regular season, the chronically dreadful Senators found themselves looking back at the pack; and at the close of this, the seventh game of the World Series, they may find themselves champions of baseball.

Poised to deny them that ultimate triumph are the New York Giants, the most consistently successful of all clubs. In the previous twenty years they have topped the National League ten times, and this is their fourth consecutive World Series appearance. Commanded by John McGraw, "The Little Napoleon" famed for his field generalship and for his tyranny over the troops, the Giants were overwhelmingly favored to take the Series when it opened last week. They had batted .300 *as a team,* their defense was strong, and their pitching was capable if not outstanding. But perhaps most important, the Giants were experienced winners.

The novice Senators are led by "Boy Wonder" Bucky Harris, a twenty-seven-year-old second baseman in his debut as a player-manager. The Nats, as they are also known, are themselves a solid-hitting club, batting .294 during the regular season—but they clouted only 22 homers. Their glovework is dependable and their pitching staff, though three starters are over thirty-five, nevertheless proved to be the most effective in the American League—thanks largely to a rookie relief sensation named Firpo Marberry and to a rejuvenated old warhorse named Walter Johnson.

Johnson, if you recall, was the freshman Senator whom the Tigers defeated on the day after that 9–9 marathon back in 1907. In the years since, that nineteen-year-old has gone on to become simply the greatest pitcher who ever lived. Backed by a generally wretched team, the big right-hander with the blazing fastball won twenty or more games in ten straight seasons, led the league in strikeouts twelve times, and was tops in shutouts on seven occasions. In his youth his fastball had gained him the nickname "The Big Train"; in recent years, as the express began to come in on the local track, he has affectionately been called "Old Barney."

Walter Johnson had given his all to the Senators through eighteen arduous seasons. This year, at the age of thirty-six, he posted a mark of 23–7, his first twenty-win performance since 1919. At last this gem of a hurler would have his chance to shine in a championship setting. The entire country was rooting for him to win a game, though fully expecting the Nats to drop the Series.

Johnson came up empty in the first game, losing 4–3 in twelve innings; and in Game Five, played in New York two days ago, he was roughed up for thirteen hits, losing 6–2. When Old Barney boarded the train back to the capital that night, he had tears in his eyes.

Washington's Griffith Stadium will be packed today, over 30,000 fans for sure. And one of them will be the President, Calvin Coolidge. The tight-lipped chief of state was not thought to be much of a fan before the Series, but he sure looks like one now. This is his third game this week. Let's make ourselves comfortable in the box next to his, between home and first. The game is still a few moments off, so while the Senators conclude infield warm-ups, have a look around this concrete-and-steel park. Griffith Stadium is named after the principal owner of the club, Clark Griffith, himself a former manager of the Senators and for years one of the craftiest pitchers in the big time. His background as a pitcher is reflected in the spacious dimensions of the playing field—402 feet down the line in left (shortened considerably this week by the addition of temporary bleachers), 421 to dead center, and 328 to the right-field foul pole. The latter provides a reasonable distance for a hitter to shoot at, but the 31-foot-high wall in right transforms many a home run into a double or loud single.

The seating capacity was boosted in 1920 through the addition of an upper deck, which until this World Series had served mostly as a sanctuary for birds and bats. You see, over the years the Washington fans had grown so accustomed to terrible baseball that they were content to read the game accounts in the papers, along with news of other calamities. So even in their pennant-winning season, the Nats drew fewer than 9,000 paying customers per home date.

The President and Mrs. Coolidge have taken their seats now —there he is in the gray fedora; she's wearing the ruffled blouse and large navy-blue bonnet—and the players have returned to their dugouts. Striding out from the bullpen in centerfield is . . . is it Walter Johnson? No, it's . . . Curly Ogden. Curly Ogden! He's a sore-armed part-timer who hasn't pitched an inning through the first six games of the Series! How can he be expected to contain the mighty Giants?

The stadium rocks with applause for the other starters as they run out to their positions. From first to third: Joe Judge, a .324 hitter this season, having an even better Series; Bucky Harris, not blessed with natural ability, but a guy who'll find a way to beat you; Ossie Bluege, regularly the third baseman, but now playing out of position because of an injury to Roger Peckinpaugh; and Tommy Taylor, a rookie with only twenty-six major-league games under his belt. In left field the Senators have Goose Goslin, the league's RBI champ and a .344 hitter; in center, Earl McNeely, a heralded rookie brought up from the minors in midseason; in right, Sam Rice, a .334 batsman and fine glove man. And the backstop is Muddy Ruel, a pretty fair hitter who has been having a terrible time of it in the Series—not even a single through the first six games.

The first hitter Ogden will face is Freddie Lindstrom, an eighteen-year-old third sacker who got his chance to play when Heinie Groh tore up his leg in September. The kid has been a star of the Series, with nine hits. Ogden fans him on three pitches—and starts to walk off the mound! But Harris, from his second-base position, waves him back. Frankie Frisch, the flashy second baseman with a .328 batting mark, draws a walk, and again Ogden strolls toward the dugout! This time Harris lets him go. He motions toward the bullpen and in comes the tall, thin, thirty-five-year-old left-hander George Mogridge. The crowd is in an uproar. What in blazes is going on?

I have some inside information on that. Last night, Bucky Harris paid a visit to Clark Griffith at his home. The young manager had an idea about how to outmaneuver the old master, John McGraw. The Giant batter whom Harris least wanted to see at the plate in the late innings was Bill Terry, a left-handed-hitting first baseman who had batted .500 through the first six games. McGraw had platooned Terry with the right-handed-hitting Irish Meusel. Against right-handed pitching, Terry would play first and George Kelly would be in center field; against lefties, Kelly would play first, Meusel would go to the outfield, and Terry would sit. Left-handed starter Tom Zachary was not available for Game Seven, since he had gone all the way to win Game Six. George Mogridge, the Senators' only other lefty, was not durable enough for Harris to count on him for going nine— and as soon as he exited, in would come Terry at perhaps the climactic point in the game. Harris's brainstorm: (a) start right-hander Curly Ogden, thus inducing McGraw to place Terry in the starting lineup; (b) allow Curly to pitch to one batter; then (c) replace him with Mogridge. McGraw, who rarely allowed Terry to face a left-hander during the regular season, would then probably yank Bill for Meusel. With Terry out of the action, Harris could counter with Marberry.

So why did Harris keep Ogden on the mound after he had retired the first batter? Bucky was simply being flexible. Maybe this was Ogden's day, he reasoned; why not let him have another roll of the dice?

But where, you ask, does Walter Johnson fit into Harris's clever plan? Sadly, he doesn't.

Mogridge struck out Ross Youngs and got George Kelly on a grounder to third to end the Giants' first. Now Washington is coming to bat, and it's time to have a look at the New Yorkers in the field. On the hill is Virgil Barnes, a slightly built, tall right-hander whose 16 wins during the season tied Jack Bentley for team honors. Older brother Jesse had pitched splendidly for the Giants in the 1921 classic, winning two games, but Virgil's Series baptism was a thrashing in Game Four. The other half of the battery is 6'2" Hank Gowdy, a fine receiver and at thirty-five the senior member of the starting nine. At first base we see converted pitcher Bill Terry, who batted a mere .239 during the season but has developed as a hitter day by day in this Series; at second, switch-hitting, slick-fielding Frankie Frisch; at short, Travis Jackson, twenty years old and in his first year as a regular; and at third, Freddie Lindstrom, possessed of a shotgun arm and extraordinary range. (The average age of the Giant infield is twenty-two!) In left there's Hack Wilson, a 5'6", 190-pound rookie, who can hit 'em a mile; in center, George "Highpockets" Kelly, so called for his 6'4" frame, five feet of which seem to be from the waist down; and in right, McGraw's favorite, Ross Youngs, a .356 hitter destined to die in his prime.

Barnes breezes through the first, getting McNeely and Rice on grounders, sandwiched around a strikeout of Harris. Indeed, Virgil sails through the entire batting order the first time around, hurling three impeccable innings. But Mogridge keeps pace. His first two batters in the second are Terry and Wilson. Both will go on to great things, particularly in 1930 when Memphis Bill will hit .401 and Hack will drive in 190 runs; but in this inning each is retired on a ground ball. (Incredibly, the first six men John McGraw has sent to the plate this afternoon will all wind up in the Hall of Fame!) Travis Jackson smacks yet another bouncer, but Taylor, the sub third baseman who broke a knuckle in his throwing hand last week, pulls Judge off the bag with his toss. The crowd stirs anxiously as old Hank Gowdy, the batting star of the 1914 World Series, follows with a single to left, but both runners are stranded as Barnes goes down swinging.

Virgil strikes out McNeely to make ten straight Senators he's retired—but then the spell is broken. Bucky Harris, who has hit only one home run all season long, measures a fastball and de-

Bill Terry was disgruntled on the days George Kelly played first, and volunteered for outfield duty. John McGraw refused, saying, "Think I want you to get hit on the head and killed?" Next year he will be the everyday first baseman and bat .319.

posits it over the temporary-bleacher wall in left for his second circuit blow of the Series. The fans, mesmerized into silence by the pitchers' duel that had been developing, erupt in a joyous explosion of cheers. In yesterday's vital win, Bucky had hit a two-run double for his team's only runs. Late-night plotting aside, his best managing of the Series has certainly been done with his bat.

With the crowd still abuzz about the home run, Sam Rice sends a soft liner out over shortstop; it looks like a sure hit, but Wilson, fleet of foot despite his fire-plug stature, races in to make a shoestring catch. Goslin grounds out, and Barnes is clearly back on the beam.

Though touched for a bunt single by Frisch in the third, Mogridge keeps the Giants off the scoreboard. In the fourth, he delights Harris by striking out Terry. This has to set John McGraw to thinking: with Mogridge looking good for the long haul, how can he continue to hold out Irish Meusel, a right-handed bruiser who in the past three seasons has averaged 120 RBI's?

Through five frames now, Big George has held the Giants at bay with only three hits. In the top of the sixth, Ross Youngs steps in, assumes his crouch stance, and poises himself "like lightning about to strike," in the words of catcher Muddy Ruel. Mogridge nibbles at the corners, but is overcareful; Youngs takes first on a free pass. As George falls behind 3–1 on the count to Kelly, the fans begin to get restless. Should Kelly take the next pitch and hope to work out the walk? What do you think? Mogridge's control seems to be slipping, and conventional strategy would be to wait him out for the walk and then move up both runners with a bunt. But McGraw does not always go "by the book." Here he figures that Mogridge will throw the ball down the middle for fear of the walk. Aggressively, he flashes the signal for the hit-and-run. With Youngs in motion on the pitch, Kelly laces a single over second and Youngs coasts into third.

The scheduled batter now is Terry—but McGraw, remembering how Mogridge had handled him in the fourth, sends up Meusel in his place. Harris runs in from second, pats Mogridge on the back, and waves to the bullpen for Fred Marberry, nicknamed Firpo for his resemblance to the Argentinian heavyweight who nearly KO'd Dempsey last year. A 6'1", 190-pound Texas strongboy with no other pitch besides the high hard one, he became the best relief pitcher of 1924, or any year prior.

Look at him out on the mound, storming around angrily, kicking his left foot up in Meusel's eyes and blazing a fastball in there. You can hear the pop in Ruel's glove anywhere in the park. But Firpo is not unhittable today. Meusel connects with a pitch and sends a fly ball to deep right, scoring Youngs. The game is tied. Wilson follows with a hit up the middle, bouncing over Marberry's head and scooting into center field. Kelly, never hesitating for a moment, makes third. There is still only one out, and the lead run can score without benefit of a base hit.

Now Washington seems to get a break—Travis Jackson tops one down to first base, and Kelly pauses midway between third and home. Even though Joe Judge fumbles the ball, to his surprise he still has a shot at nailing Kelly, who is racing for the plate. However, Judge freezes with indecision: should he throw home or make the play at first base? If he tries for Kelly and fails, the floodgates may be opened for a really big inning; yet if he chooses to get the sure out at first base, he'll be conceding what may be the run that decides the championship of the world. While Judge weighs the options, Kelly comes in to score, Wilson takes second base, and Jackson crosses first.

The next play proves equally distressing, as Gowdy's perfect double-play grounder handcuffs shortstop Bluege and dribbles into left field. Wilson comes home and Jackson takes third base.

Firpo Marberry is the game's first frightening relief pitcher. Like Rich Gossage in years to come, he puts everything he has into a pitch, throwing only heat. He was five years in the majors before throwing his first curve.

An audible sigh fills the stadium.

Virgil Barnes, an awful batsman even for a pitcher, is at the plate now. If he gets a hit we can all go home. Marberry rears back and fires, and Barnes connects—but the ball comes down softly in the glove of Sam Rice, in very short right field, and Jackson must hold at third. Lindstrom takes strike three, and the Giants are finally out. The score is 3–1.

The way Barnes is going, that lead looks plenty big enough. He puts the Nats down without a peep in the bottom of the sixth. He has now retired eighteen of the nineteen men he's faced. If Washington is to maintain even a glimmer of optimism, Marberry must hold the fort—which he does, not permitting a hit in the seventh or eighth while fanning two. The Senators, in the meantime, rouse themselves in their half of the seventh as Harris beats out a hit to deep short. But then Rice raps into a double play, and Goslin's single which follows is to no avail.

The home eighth commences bleakly as Bluege lifts a foul pop to Gowdy. Only five outs stand between the Giants and the world championship. Tommy Taylor is due up, but Harris looks down his bench for a more potent bat. Out comes Nemo Leibold, a veteran "Punch-and-Judy" hitter who has been blanked in his five at bats in the Series. This time, Little Nemo awakes from Slumberland and slaps a pitch down the third-base line. The ball grazes the bag on its way into left field, and Leibold reaches second standing up. As Muddy Ruel, 0-for-18, readies to "try, try again," the fans groan. Why can't Bucky send up somebody else, *anybody* else? But Ruel silences the doubters; he singles up the right-field line, with Kelly making a fine play to knock the ball down and keep Leibold at third. Batting for Marberry now is Bennie Tate, who has appeared twice in the Series, both times as a pinch hitter, and twice has drawn a walk. Barnes has enjoyed perfect control to this point, yet he, too, comes under the mysterious influence of Mr. Tate and provides him with a pass. This loads the bases for Earl McNeely, the twenty-five-year-old rookie whose mid-July purchase cost Washington $50,000. He disappoints mightily by lining to left, not deep enough for Leibold to challenge Meusel's arm.

Now it's Bucky Harris's turn at bat. No one else has driven in a run for Washington these last two games—can he do it again? Hank Gowdy calls time and runs to the bench to confer with John McGraw, but mere words of wisdom will not alter destiny. Harris hits a seemingly routine grounder to Lindstrom; but on its last bound before settling into Freddie's glove, the ball strikes a pebble and soars a foot over his head. As Meusel runs over to retrieve the ball, Leibold and Ruel score, and bedlam reigns. Poor Virgil Barnes, good but not lucky, hands the ball over to McGraw and heads for the clubhouse. His replacement is left-handed Art Nehf, a top-notch starter who won the opener and lost a tough one yesterday. He retires Sam Rice on a grounder to Kelly, and the inning ends with two Senators left on base.

As loud a roar as we heard when Harris hit that single, it was puny compared to the joyous noise which surrounds us now. For walking to the mound in the smoke and the haze of the rapidly setting sun is . . . Walter Johnson! He hadn't wanted Bucky to use him in a tight spot just because of sentiment, and risk blowing the Series for the whole team. But Bucky came to him as the eighth inning ended and said simply, "You're the best we've got, Walter . . . we'll win or lose with you."

Throwing in his warm-ups, Johnson knows he is not the same pitcher who once won 68 games in two years, whose fastball had caused Sam Crawford to moan, "You can't see it; all you can do is hear it go by you." Johnson later will tell reporters that what he was thinking as he took the mound was, "I'll need the breaks."

The first man Walter has to face in the ninth is Lindstrom, who cracked four hits off him the last time they'd squared off. But today is another day. Freddie pops to Ralph Miller, now playing third in place of Thomas. Next up is Frisch, "The Fordham Flash," who at twenty-one had gone straight from the Rose Hill campus to the Giants' starting lineup. Frankie smashes a Johnson fastball to deep, deep center. McNeely races back toward the wall, but the ball is beyond him. By the time he gets it back into the infield, Frisch is standing on third.

With gloom weighting the air, Harris now orders an intentional walk to left-handed-hitting Youngs. Kelly, a righty, is to follow. Harris has made the classic "percentage" move, so called because of the proven statistical advantage that pitch-

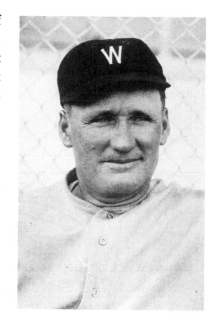

Walter Johnson

ers enjoy when facing a same-side batter. But has he forgotten that in Game One "Highpockets" belted a home run off Johnson?

On the first pitch to Kelly, a strike, Youngs breaks for second. Ruel bluffs a throw, hoping to draw Frisch down the line from third and trap him. Frankie doesn't take the bait, and now two runners are in scoring position with only one out. Unfazed, Johnson makes Harris look like a genius as he throws strike two and strike three by Kelly. Meusel follows with a tame ground ball to Miller, and the threat is over.

In the bottom of the ninth, it's Washington's turn to put the pressure on: After Goslin bounces to Frisch, Judge singles.

Bluege's grounder is swept up by Kelly, who throws to second—but Travis Jackson, late covering the bag, drops the throw. Bluege is safe at first, and Judge advances to third. With only one down, the batter is Ralph Miller, an unlikely hero—he played in only nine games for the Senators in 1924, and sported a batting average of .133. Nonetheless, McGraw is nervous enough to yank Nehf and replace him with righty Hugh McQuillan (again a percentage move). McGraw's masterminding proves every bit the equal of his counterpart's, as Miller grounds to Jackson, who throws to Frisch for one out and on to Kelly for the inning-ending, game-saving double play.

Extra innings! Only once before, in 1912, did the seventh and final game of the World Series extend past the regulation nine, and it hasn't happened since. Johnson walks Hack Wilson to open the tenth, but gets Jackson on a called strike three. Gowdy raps one back to Walter, whose throw to Bluege initiates a double play on the leaden-footed catcher. The home half commences with Ruel grounding to Frisch. Johnson, up next, belts a tremendous drive to left center. Will it go out? Everyone in the stadium is standing now as the ball nears the wall, but it is caught by Wilson. Oh, well—that ending would have been *too* storybook-style. Relative calm is restored, and McNeely fans.

McQuillan is due to lead off the Giant eleventh, but McGraw puts up a surprise pinch hitter: the crippled Heinie Groh, whom we saw in the double no-hit game seven years back. Heinie has not yet seen action in this Series, but he has not forgotten how to flick that bottle bat. He drives a single to short right, then exits for a pinch runner. Lindstrom sacrifices, and Old Barney is in trouble again. Reaching back for his fastball of old, he throws three pitches to the dangerous Frisch, who swings three times and sits back down. Again Youngs is deliberately passed, and again Kelly strikes out. What a performance!

The first two Nats up in the eleventh are disposed of by Jack

Bentley, the left-handed ace of the staff who defeated Johnson in Game Five. But then Goslin stirs up trouble by dumping a Texas League double in left center. McGraw takes a cue from Harris and passes Judge intentionally; he also directs Meusel and Youngs to switch outfield positions, moving Youngs's stronger arm into left with the right-handed Bluege up. Bluege, dizzy from all the strategy going on around him, simply grounds into a force.

The sustained drama and tension of the last six innings have been almost unbearable. Look around at the fans—except for the President, who is utterly unflappable, the rest of us look and feel like wrung-out wash. Irish Meusel singles to right in the twelfth, and here we go again; Johnson has not had an easy inning yet. But with each thrust by the Giants he parries one better. This time he strikes out Wilson, induces Jackson to hit a force-out grounder, and gets Gowdy on a fly.

The best has been saved for last.

McGraw returns Meusel to left and Youngs to right, the momentary crisis having passed. Miller is up first, but he can't get a rally started, grounding out to Frisch. Muddy Ruel follows with a high foul not far behind the plate, the kind of chance Hank Gowdy has been handling with ease for thirteen years—but not today. In a strange lapse of judgment, instead of tossing his mask behind him as all catchers are instructed to do, Hank flips it a few steps *ahead* of him. Pursuing the ball, he steps squarely into the mask. He kicks it off, then incredibly steps into it a *second* time! The spikes of his shoes are now stuck in the wires of the mask, and he cannot get free. Trying to pursue the ball with the mask on one foot, he finally stumbles as the ball falls to earth a few feet from where he does. Reprieved, Ruel—batting .050 for the Series—doubles past third base.

Next is Walter Johnson. Time for a pinch hitter? No, Harris is going down the line with Walter, who raps a grounder to short.

Ruel runs at Jackson as the ball is hit, trying to distract him by decoying a dash for third. Then as Ruel stops and prepares to backtrack to second, Jackson fumbles the ball and both runners are safe.

The batter is Earl McNeely, 0-for-5 today with two strikeouts. Can he do it? Apparently not, as he hits a hard bouncer to Lindstrom, perfect for a double play. But as Lindstrom crouches for the grab, the ball strikes a pebble—perhaps the *same* pebble which aided Harris's grounder in the eighth—and rockets over Freddie's head into left. Meusel's racing in for the ball . . . Ruel's steaming around third . . . there'll be no play! Ruel crosses the plate and the Washington fans go wild, pouring out onto the field by the thousands. As McNeely touches first base, he is surrounded by fans who put him up on their shoulders and carry him around like a trophy. Other Senators are grabbed, jabbed, thumped, bumped, and manhandled by the adoring throng. Only the assistance of police enables some players to evade the clutches of their admirers. In the outfield people are jumping, dancing, turning cartwheels for joy. Hats are being tossed into the air like so much confetti. Washington has done it! Johnson has done it!

Even Calvin Coolidge looks pleased.

October 10, 1924

NEW YORK

	AB	R	H	P	A	E
Lindstrom, 3b.	5	0	1	0	3	0
Frisch, 2b.	5	0	2	3	4	0
Youngs, rf.-lf.	2	1	0	2	0	0
Kelly, cf.-1b.	6	1	1	8	1	0
Terry, 1b.	2	0	0	6	1	0
a Meusel, lf.-rf. ...	3	0	1	1	0	0
Wilson, lf.-cf.	5	1	1	4	0	0
Jackson, ss.	6	0	0	1	4	2
Gowdy, c.	6	0	1	8	0	1
Barnes, p.	4	0	0	1	2	0
Nehf, p.	0	0	0	0	0	0
McQuillan, p.	0	0	0	0	0	0
e Groh	1	0	1	0	0	0
f Southworth	0	0	0	0	0	0
Bentley, p.	0	0	0	0	0	0
TOTALS	45	3	8	34	15	3

WASHINGTON

	AB	R	H	P	A	E
McNeely, cf.	6	0	1	0	0	0
Harris, 2b.	5	1	3	4	1	0
Rice, rf.	5	0	0	2	0	0
Goslin, lf.	5	0	2	3	0	0
Judge, 1b.	4	0	1	11	1	1
Bluege, ss.	5	0	0	1	7	2
Taylor, 3b.	2	0	0	0	3	1
b Leibold	1	1	1	0	0	0
Miller, 3b.	2	0	0	1	1	0
Ruel, c.	5	2	2	13	0	0
Ogden, p.	0	0	0	0	0	0
Mogridge, p.	1	0	0	0	0	0
Marberry, p.	1	0	0	1	0	0
c Tate	0	0	0	0	0	0
d Shirley	0	0	0	0	0	0
Johnson, p.	2	0	0	0	1	0
TOTALS	44	4	10	36	14	4

a Flied out for Terry in 6th
b Doubled for Taylor in 8th
c Walked for Marberry in 8th
d Ran for Tate in 8th
e Singled for McQuillan in 11th
f Ran for Groh in 11th

```
NEW YORK       000  003  000  000 — 3
WASHINGTON     000  100  020  001 — 4
```

RBI—Meusel, Harris 3, McNeely. 2B—Goslin, Leibold, Lindstrom, McNeely, Ruel. 3B—Frisch. HR—Harris. SB—Youngs. Sac.—Lindstrom. Sac. Fly—Meusel. DP—N.Y. 2, Wash. 1. LOB—N.Y. 14, Wash. 8. Umpires—Dinneen, Quigley, Connolly, Klem. Time—3:00. Att.—31,667.

NEW YORK	IP	H	R	ER	BB	SO
Barnes	7⅔	6	3	3	1	6
Nehf	⅔	1	0	0	0	0
McQuillan	1⅔	0	0	0	0	1
Bentley (L)	1⅓	3	1	1	1	0

WASHINGTON						
Ogden	⅓	0	0	0	1	1
Mogridge	4⅔	4	2	1	1	3
Marberry	3	1	1	0	1	3
Johnson(W)	4	3	0	0	3	5

New York Giants vs. Washington Senators   59

October 12, 1929
Chicago Cubs
vs.
Philadelphia A's

Let's go to another World Series game, one with perhaps not so spine-tingling a setting. This afternoon's contest is not Game Seven but Game Four, and it does not pit David against Goliath: Both teams are powerhouses, having coasted to their league titles, and both are old hands at postseason play.

Sounds like a nice, relaxing couple of hours in the sun, doesn't it? Don't sink back in your seat—you're about to see the most surprising and explosive game in World Series history.

We find ourselves in Philadelphia again, twenty-two years after that wild tie game with the Tigers. But we are not in Columbia Park. That ramshackle structure has long since vanished, replaced by Shibe Park, first of the concrete-and-steel stadiums, named after the A's owner who had it built. And the players who thrilled us back then have vanished, too, all except one: Remember the kid who hit an insignificant pinch single in the final inning? Now forty-four and in his twenty-fourth big-league campaign, the great Eddie Collins does not play in the field anymore but, coming full circle, pinch-hits now and then. However, the main link between the A's of 1907 and the team we will see this afternoon is Cornelius Alexander McGillicuddy, also known as Connie Mack. The grand old man of baseball began managing in the majors in 1894 and will still be at it in 1950, his fiftieth consecutive year at the Philadelphia helm.

Though Connie could not lead his boys past the Tigers in 1907–09, the A's took the flag in four of the next five years. After a shocking loss to the Braves in the 1914 World Series, though, Mack dismantled his marvelous team and proceeded to finish dead last in each of the next seven years! Not until this season did they finish on top again, exploding past the "Murderers Row" Yankees of Ruth, Gehrig, and Lazzeri to win the pennant by a whopping eighteen games! These 1929 A's are *some* team, with hitters like Jimmie Foxx, Al Simmons, and Mickey Cochrane and a pitching staff led by Lefty Grove and George Earnshaw.

You'd think an opponent would need courage just to step out on the field with them. But the Chicago Cubs are loaded, too. Completely revamped since we last saw them in 1917, the Cubs romped to the National League flag by ten and a half games. Managed by Joe McCarthy, they coupled good pitchers like Pat Malone, Charlie Root, and Guy Bush with one of the most awesome right-handed-hitting attacks baseball has ever seen: Rogers Hornsby, Kiki Cuyler, Riggs Stephenson, and Hack Wilson, who combined for a batting average of .362!

That right-handed power convinced Connie Mack to hold Lefty Grove and Rube Walberg, his two left-handed starters, out of the rotation for the Series. Opening at Chicago's Wrigley Field, the A's took Game One as right-hander Howard Ehmke, a forgotten man during the regular season, baffled the Cubs with his sidearm slants. In Game Two the A's scored nine runs to back up the combined mound efforts of Earnshaw and Grove. Chicago's situation would be desperate today had Guy Bush not come through with a 3–1 win in the opener at Shibe Park. Still, the Cubs must win one more here in Philadelphia or it could be over in five.

It is a dazzlingly perfect fall day, with a sparkling azure sky, gentle breezes, a strong warming sun. Shibe Park is filled to its capacity of 29,921 fans. Let's enter by the gate on Somerset Street and find two places in the left-field stands, where we can catch the sun's rays for the whole game. Having enjoyed such good fortune with thirty-five-year-old Ehmke, Mr. Mack will today try *forty-five-year-old* Jack Quinn. Unlike fellow gray-beard Eddie Collins, who, though on the active roster, seldom stirs from the bench, Quinn hurled 161 innings in 1929, posting a record of 11–9. He joined the New York Highlanders in 1909 at age twenty-five, and after a poor showing in 1912 was returned to the minors as "too old" to improve. Ha! This medical marvel will still be pitching in the big time at the age of forty-nine.

Look at him throw in his warm-ups. His fingers go to his mouth before every pitch. Isn't throwing a spitball in 1929 against the rules, you ask? Yes—but not for Quinn. You see, in 1920, when the spitball and other "unfair" pitches (emery ball, mudball, shineball, etc.) were officially banned, seventeen hurlers were permitted to continue throwing the wet one because it was deemed essential to their livelihoods. Of these seventeen, only four are still active, and one of these is Jack Quinn.

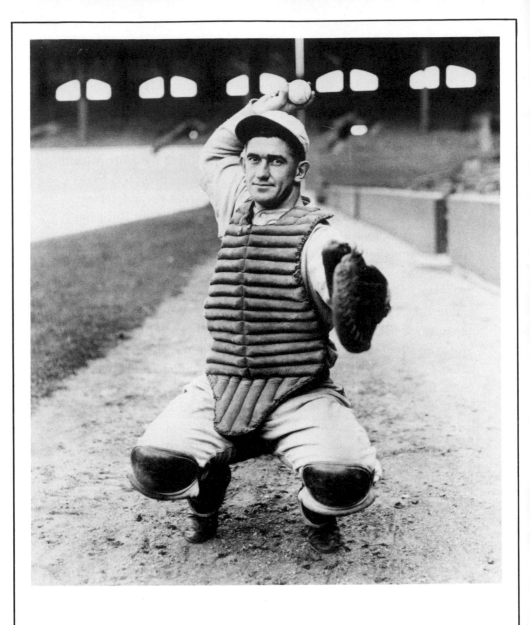

Besides being a great defensive backstop, Mickey Cochrane hit .331 this year; he will hit .357 next year; and .349 the year after that. When he hangs up his spikes in 1937, he will have the highest lifetime average of any catcher.

He indulges in one last pregame toss, the infielders whip the ball around one last time, and the A's man their positions. Behind the plate is Mickey Cochrane, who can do it all: hit, run, catch, throw. The twenty-one-year-old strongboy Jimmie Foxx, marked for greatness, is at first; "Camera Eye" Max Bishop, so named for his ability to draw walks, is at second; Joe Boley, a late bloomer who didn't hit the big time till he was thirty, is at short; and Jimmy Dykes, a scrapper in his twelfth season with the A's, and having his best year, is at third. Standing beneath us in left is Aloysius Harry Szymanski—Al Simmons to you—a .334 lifetime hitter who hits savage line drives. Out in center is Mule Haas, whose .313 average is only sixth best in this club. And over there in right is Bing Miller, a fine all-around player whose brother Ralph we saw in the 1924 Series.

Stepping into the batter's box is Norm McMillan, the Cub third baseman who has had only one hit through the first three games. Quinn throws four pitches, can't find the plate with any of them, and McMillan trots contentedly to first. Next up is Woody English, the twenty-two-year-old shortstop. Play for one run and bunt? Not with the lumber that follows in this lineup. English swings, lifting a fly ball to right which Miller nabs in foul ground. Now Quinn must contend with Rogers Hornsby, the greatest right-handed hitter in history. In 1929, his first year with the Cubs, Hornsby was named Most Valuable Player in the National League. Pitching carefully, Quinn runs the count to 3–2, then loads up his juiciest spitter and fans the Rajah. The next batter is no slouch, either: Hack Wilson, whom the Cubs spirited away in 1925 when the Giants foolishly exposed him to the minor-league draft. He smacks a single to right, English holding at second. Kiki Cuyler, third of the Cubs' fearsome right-handed foursome, was another great acquisition, picked up from the Pirates in 1927. He hit a mere .360 this year. At this point in today's game, however, he strikes out.

Taking the mound for the Cubs is right-hander Charlie Root,

19–6 during the league season. In the opening contest four days ago he pitched splendidly in defeat, allowing only three hits and one run in seven innings. His battery mate is Zack Taylor, a ten-year veteran picked up from the Braves in July when it became clear that Gabby Hartnett's sore arm would prevent him from catching this season. McMillan is at third, English—the only one of the starters who came to the majors as a Cub—is at short, Hornsby at second, and Charley Grimm at first. "Jolly Cholly," as this banjo-playing, life-of-the-party type is known, is the team's lone left-handed swinger. The right fielder is Cuyler, the center fielder is Wilson, and in left is Riggs Stephenson, formerly an infielder with the Cleveland Indians, whose fourteen-year career will leave him with an average of .336.

First of the Athletics to face Root is Max Bishop, whose fine judgment at the plate this year produced 128 bases on balls, a remarkable total for a fellow who hit a mere .232. Max waits on Root till he can wait no more, then lifts a soft fly to left. Mule Haas dribbles one down to McMillan for out number two, and "Black Mike" Cochrane pops to English to conclude this tame half-inning.

Quinn and Root both have an easy time of it in the second, putting the side down one, two, three, but in the third, each must struggle a bit. Root drives a hard grounder toward the hole between short and third; Boley makes a great one-handed stop, plant, turn, and throw to record the out. McMillan fouls to Foxx, but Quinn walks English, a real no-no, for it allows Hornsby to bat with a man on. Though the Rajah grounds out to short to end the inning, Quinn has given signs that he is not as sharp as he'll need to be against this lineup. Root's trouble begins with Jimmy Dykes, who singles to right and goes to second as Cuyler bobbles the ball. In a move of questionable wisdom, with Quinn up next, Boley sacrifices Dykes to third. But Quinn fans and Bishop grounds out, and we move on to the fourth.

Hack Wilson presents an odd sight strutting to the plate: at 5′6″ and 190 pounds, with a size 18 collar and size 5½ shoe, he is both monumental and miniature. But with a bat in his hands he is simply Herculean, whipping his massive arms in a devastatingly forceful arc. Opening the fourth, he blasts the ball to deep right, but Miller backs to the warning track and gloves it. Cuyler follows with another opposite-field smash, this one a single past first base that Miller lets skip through him. Cuyler makes third base, but cannot tag up and score as Quinn gets Stephenson on an infield pop. That was the big out, as once again Quinn passed through the fearsome foursome unscathed. But perhaps growing careless, Quinn provides a belt-high fastball to Grimm, who parks it over the right-field wall for two runs.

In the A's half, after one out Cochrane loops a double to left. Up comes "Bucketfoot" Al Simmons, itching to belt one downtown. The pitch comes in, he raises his left foot ("stepping into the bucket," it's called, because it looks like the hitter is heading for the bench, where the water bucket is), and swings. But Al beats the ball in the ground to McMillan, who sees Cochrane too far off second and throws to Hornsby for the out. Foxx ends the threat with a drive to deep left center which Wilson runs down.

Quinn recovers in the fifth and breezes past the Bearcubs on three infield plays, but Root again teeters on the brink. Bing Miller hits one back through the box, deflecting off Root's glove, for a single. Dykes sends a routine fly to center; inexplicably, Wilson muffs it. With runners on first and second, no one out, and Joe Boley at the plate, the A's attempt a double steal—but Taylor's throw to third nails Miller. Boley blasts one to right center, where Wilson atones for his error by making a fine running one-hand catch near the scoreboard. Quinn, as he did in the third inning, strikes out.

It is the top of the sixth now in what is shaping up as a

Hack Wilson—when he hit 'em, they traveled.

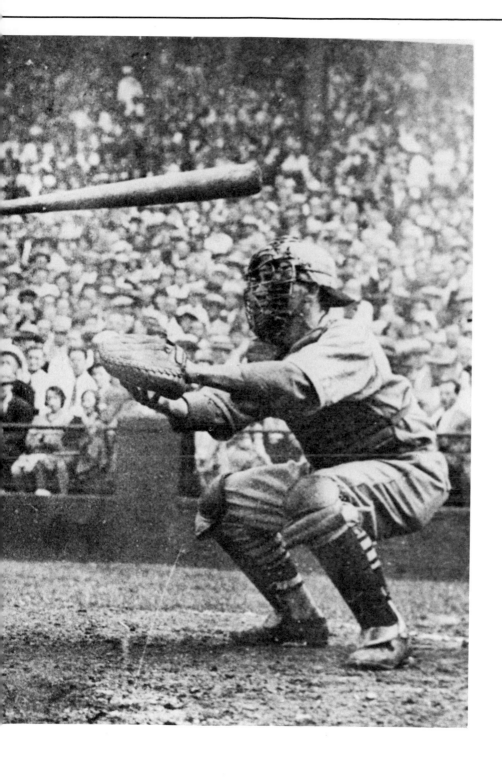

pitchers' duel. Scheduled to bat is the heart of the Cubs' order, beginning with Hornsby. In addition to hitting for a lifetime average of .358, second only to Cobb, from 1921 through 1925 the Rajah had an astronomical batting average of .408! Still, his cantankerous personality put him in such frequent opposition to his bosses that he played for four teams in four years. Hitless in his first two trips against Quinn, Hornsby this time rips a single to center. Wilson follows with a single to right. Cuyler singles to center. Stephenson singles in the infield. Machine-gun style, the fearsome foursome have riddled Quinn for two runs and have driven him from the mound. In comes Rube Walberg, a lefty who won 18 games for the A's this year. Grimm bunts to the left of the mound. Walberg's hurried throw sails into the box seats behind first base; Cholly, credited with a single, goes to third, and Cuyler and Stephenson score. Fans moaned and groaned as hit followed fast upon hit, but this messed-up play has taken the life out of them. You could hear that proverbial pin drop in Shibe Park as Zack Taylor's fly to Haas brings in the fifth and final run of the inning. Mercifully for the Philadelphia faithful, Root and McMillan fan to end this disastrous top of the sixth.

Root comes out firing with that 7–0 lead. He knows this is no time to get cute and walk somebody—just put the ball over the plate and let them hit it. Bishop, Haas, and Cochrane go down quickly and quietly, and now the disheartened fans can only hope there is no further carnage in the seventh.

But there is. Knuckleballer Eddie Rommel, a 27-game winner as a starter in 1922 and a fine reliever in '29, takes the hill in place of Walberg. His first batter, English, goes out on a short fly to center. Next is Hornsby, who pounces on a knuckler that doesn't knuckle and drives it far over Haas's head for a triple. Cuyler singles to left for his third hit of the game, and we are at 8–0 and still counting; the Series will be all even at two games apiece. But this will not be another big inning. Stephenson grounds to Dykes, who goes around the horn for the double play.

Connie Mack studies his lineup card as the A's jog to the bench for the bottom of the seventh; after the regulars take their licks, he intends to substitute en masse, so that in years to come, even the lowliest scrub on the team can say, "I played in the World Series." As the fans rise for the traditional seventh-inning stretch, some prudent ones make for the exits to beat the rush. So why are *we* staying? And why did I bring you to a wipeout game like this one, anyway? Patience, patience!

The sun still blazes brightly as it hovers just above the stands in back of home. Al Simmons is the first Athletic up in the bottom of the seventh, and he gets all of a Root fastball, launching it over the stands and onto the roof in left. A smattering of applause greets this prodigious blow. "At least we won't get shut out," is the reaction on the A's bench. Up comes Jimmie Foxx, who three years from now will belt 58 home runs, but today has been blanked by Root. "Double X" singles to right. Bing Miller follows with a catchable liner to center. Wilson takes one step in, then freezes—he has lost sight of the ball in the sun, and it drops in front of him for a single. Foxx, thinking the ball would be caught, can advance no farther than second. Jimmy Dykes whips another single into left, scoring Foxx and pushing Miller to second. Mack senses that Root is losing his stuff, and tells Boley to swing at the first pitch that's even close to the plate. Boley does as he is told, and singles to right, bringing Miller home and sending Dykes to third. The crowd is stirring now: the outcome of the game is surely not in doubt, but at least the A's are showing a little life.

Mack calls on George Burns to bat for Rommel. Only three years ago the American League's MVP, Burns is now in the twilight of his career. Hitless in seventeen pinch-hit attempts during the season, he fares no better against Root, popping to English for the first out of the inning. But Bishop resumes the staccato of singles, returning a pitch back through the box to bring in Dykes. The crowd leaps to its feet, roaring, daring to think the impossible.

The score has narrowed to 8–4 and A's stand on first and second. Joe McCarthy reaches the same conclusion as Mack and furloughs Root. Waved in from the bullpen is Art Nehf, who pitched for the Giants in the 1924 Series finale. McCarthy hopes the little lefty can stymie left-handed batters Haas and Cochrane and put an end to the rally. While taking his warm-up pitches, Nehf loses sight of the catcher's return toss and wraps his arms about his head as the ball sails out to second base. That sun is really wicked now.

Haas greets Nehf with a whistling drive to center. Uncertainly, Wilson drifts in a step or two—can't he see that the ball will go over his head? No. Hack doesn't have a clue where the ball is, having lost it in the sun just as he did Miller's drive. The ball zooms over Wilson's head and rolls all the way to the 447-foot mark in center field. Boley scores! Bishop scores! The joint is jumping. And here comes Haas around third as the ball comes back in. He slides . . . and makes it, an inside-the-park three-run homer! Leaning out of the dugout, the A's explode as Haas hits the plate. "We're back in the game, boys!" yells Jimmy Dykes, giving the teammate next to him a sound slap on the back. Only it isn't a teammate; it is Connie Mack, who goes sprawling out over the bats arrayed in front of the dugout. Mortified, Jimmy apologizes, but Mack is too happy at this moment to take offense.

In a matter of moments, Chicago's eight-run lead has been pared to one. There is still time for the Cubs to regroup forces, but Nehf walks Cochrane. With Simmons and Foxx coming up for the second time in the inning, McCarthy calls in right-handed Sheriff Blake to replace Nehf. Blake, the Cubs' fourth starter all year long, looks to be out of the inning as Simmons grounds to third. But nothing goes right for the Cubs in this inning; the perfect double-play ball takes a bad hop off McMillan's shoulder into left field, Cochrane going to second. Foxx drills a hit to center, and the once insurmountable lead is totally wiped out, a memory.

With Simmons, the lead run, poised on third, the tie is in considerable peril, and McCarthy retraces his steps to the mound. The skipper takes the ball from Blake and entrusts it to Pat Malone, the top pitcher in the National League this past year with 22 victories. The beefy right-hander immediately removes any margin for error, hitting Miller with a pitch to fill the bases. Can Big Pat draw the line here and hold it? The man he must retire is Jimmy Dykes, who singled a run home earlier in the inning. Malone's first pitch is a fastball; Dykes swings and misses. So is the next pitch, but Malone has gone to the well once too often: Dykes drives the ball to deep left, backing Riggs Stephenson against the wall. He leaps; the ball hits his glove, but is jarred loose as he makes impact with the wall. Simmons and Foxx tear around the bases to score, Miller reaches third, and Dykes pulls into second.

Ten men have crossed the plate. The A's and their admirers are delirious. The Cubs are stunned. Malone bravely keeps his composure, striking out Boley and Burns, and this unbelievable inning is over. Fifteen A's have come to the plate, and ten of them have hit safely. Turning the contest around completely, the A's seventh inning provides the perfect illustration of Yogi Berra's axiom: "A game ain't over till it's over."

In fact, it's hard to realize that even this game is not over— that Chicago, while it no longer leads by eight, still trails by only two. But the Cubs are completely demoralized, and the sight of Lefty Grove marching in from the pen can do little to lift their spirits. The phenomenal Grove, like his left-handed

Lefty Grove

predecessor with the A's, Rube Waddell, leads the American League in strikeouts year after year and in the next two seasons he will win 59 games against only 9 losses!

Jolly Cholly Grimm, like his teammates more grim than jolly, grounds to short. The next four Cubs to come up, two in the eighth and two in the ninth, will not fare even as well, going down on strikes; and Hornsby will end matters by flying out to right. The A's, in their half of the eighth, were kept off the scoreboard only because Stephenson threw Cochrane out at the plate. Tomorrow, lightning will wait till the ninth to strike: Pat Malone's 2–0 lead will evaporate as the A's score three to wrap up the Series.

As we file out of Shibe Park this afternoon, think back to those "prudent" fans who left early to beat the rush. For the rest of their lives, they will have to explain how they managed to attend this game yet miss the greatest rally in World Series history. Next time your favorite team trails by a lopsided score in the late going, before you race to be first in the parking lot or turn off the television in disgust, recall the game we saw this Columbus Day, 1929.

October 12, 1929

CHICAGO

	AB	R	H	P	A	E
McMillan, 3b.	4	0	0	1	3	0
English, ss.	4	0	0	2	1	0
Hornsby, 2b.	5	2	2	1	1	0
Wilson, cf.	3	1	2	3	0	1
Cuyler, rf.	4	2	3	0	0	1
Stephenson, lf. ...	4	1	1	2	1	0
Grimm, 1b.	4	2	2	7	0	0
Taylor, c.	3	0	0	8	1	0
Root, p.	3	0	0	0	0	0
Nehf, p.	0	0	0	0	0	0
Blake, p.	0	0	0	0	0	0
Malone, p.	0	0	0	0	0	0
b Hartnett	1	0	0	0	0	0
Carlson, p.	0	0	0	0	1	0
TOTALS	35	8	10	24	8	2

PHILADELPHIA

	AB	R	H	P	A	E
Bishop, 2b.	5	1	2	2	3	0
Haas, cf.	4	1	1	2	0	0
Cochrane, c.	4	1	2	9	0	0
Simmons, lf.	5	2	2	0	0	0
Foxx, 1b.	4	2	2	10	0	0
Miller, rf.	3	1	2	3	0	1
Dykes, 3b.	4	1	3	0	2	0
Boley, ss.	3	1	1	1	5	0
Quinn, p.	2	0	0	0	0	0
Walberg, p.	0	0	0	0	0	1
Rommel, p.	0	0	0	0	0	0
a Burns	2	0	0	0	0	0
Grove, p.	0	0	0	0	0	0
TOTALS	36	10	15	27	10	2

a Popped out and struck out for Rommel in 7th
b Struck out for Malone in 8th

CHICAGO	000	205	1 0 0 —	8
PHILADELPHIA	000	000	1 0 0 x —	10

RBI—Cuyler 2, Stephenson, Grimm 2, Taylor, Bishop, Haas 3, Simmons, Foxx, Dykes 3, Boley. 2B—Cochrane, Dykes. 3B—Hornsby. HR—Grimm, Simmons, Haas. Sac.—Boley, Haas. Sac. Fly—Taylor. DP—Phl. 1. LOB—Chi. 4, Phi. 6. Umpires—VanGratlan, Klem, Dinneen, Moran. Time—2:12. Att.—29,921.

CHICAGO	IP	H	R	ER	BB	SO
Root	6⅓	9	6	6	0	3
**Nehf	0	1	2	2	1	0
***Blake (L)	0	2	2	2	0	0
Malone	⅔	1	0	0	0	2
Carlson	1	2	0	0	0	1
PHILADELPHIA						
*Quinn	5	7	6	5	2	2
Walberg	1	1	1	0	0	2
Rommel (W)	1	2	1	1	1	0
Grove (Save)	2	0	0	0	0	4

*Pitched to four batters in 6th
**Pitched to two batters in 7th
***Pitched to two batters in 7th
HBP—Malone (1)

Chicago Cubs vs. Philadelphia A's   75

October 3, 1951
Brooklyn Dodgers
vs.
New York Giants

Here we are, some twenty-two years later, sitting in the lower left-field stands of New York's Polo Grounds, about to witness a game no schedulemaker had planned last winter, and no fan had dared to dream of even six weeks ago. The contest to be played on this dim, overcast afternoon will determine the National League champion.

The New York Giants and the Brooklyn Dodgers, who through the years have produced baseball's greatest rivalry, have this year produced baseball's greatest pennant race. While Brooklyn, which was nipped for the flag on the final day in 1950, broke fast from the starting gate, the Giants stumbled, dropping eleven straight games in April. Eventually the New Yorkers picked up the pace and moved into second place; but by August 11 they were still hopelessly behind by thirteen-and-a-half games. On the next day, however, a whirlwind began to take shape: the Giants went on to win sixteen games in a row and an unbelievable thirty-seven of their final forty-four. They pulled into a tie with two games left to play, and only a fourteenth-inning homer by Jackie Robinson against the Phils on the final day of the regular season prevented the Giants from taking the flag. In the best-of-three play-off the Giants took the first game, 3–1, and the Dodgers, with their backs to the wall, captured the second game, 10–0. Now the teams have arrived at a crossroads: After today's game, one club will meet the Yankees in a "Subway Series"; the other will lick its wounds and wait till next year.

The morning threat of rain appears to have held down the size of the crowd. Game time, 1:30, is only a few moments off, yet fewer than 35,000 people occupy this grand old cavern of a stadium, which has accommodated more than 60,000. The Polo Grounds, named after polo fields which existed on this site in the nineteenth century, may be great for football, or soccer, or even polo . . . but baseball? Look around the outfield and you'll see why this park built on Coogan's Bluff has been such a night-mare to pitchers and batters alike. Down the lines, a ball must drift a mere 258 feet to right field or 280 feet to left to become a four-bagger, dimensions which have yielded countless pop-fly homers. (Actually, a fly hit to left may travel even less than 280 feet and still be a homer, for the upper deck juts out over the stands below.) To the power alleys, where most well-hit shots go, a ball can rocket 425 feet to left center or 450 feet to right center and still be caught. Dead center is beyond home-run consideration, an outlandish 475 feet from home plate.

In mid-1948 Leo Durocher, manager of the Dodgers since 1939, was let go and, miracle of miracles, was hired by the

Giants. He inherited a team which had been designed to take advantage of the short porches in right and left—lumbering strongboys who could powder the ball but do little else. Gradually, he stripped the Giants of their aging sluggers and constructed his team around a stingy pitching crew and aggressive players who could "execute"—who could manufacture runs from such odds and ends as a grounder hit behind the runner, a bunt, a steal, or a hit-and-run, as well as the occasional circuit blast. It is these new-breed Giants who are running out to their positions now.

The big change Durocher has wrought in this team has been up the middle, where tradition has it that pennants are won or lost; so let's check out those five vital stations first. Behind the plate is Wes Westrum, an excellent receiver whose anemic batting average of .219 masks his real contributions to the team offense: 20 homers, 70 RBI's, and 102 bases on balls, all excellent totals for an eighth-place batter. Warming up on the hill is thirty-four-year-old Sal "The Barber" Maglie—his intimidating combination of fastballs up and in and curves low and away have produced 23 wins coming into today's game. Durocher reclaimed this veteran from the Mexican League last year and put him in the starting rotation with Larry Jansen, Dave Koslo, and Jim Hearn to give the New Yorkers the best moundwork in either league.

The keystone pair of Alvin Dark at short and Eddie Stanky at second was acquired as a unit in a trade with the Boston Braves, and these two scrappers have led by example in the field and molded the team spirit off the field. At thirty-five years of age Stanky, nicknamed "The Brat" for his combative nature, does not run, field, throw, or hit particularly well; but like Bucky Harris back in 1924, he finds a way to beat you. Dark, who bats second behind Stanky, is more naturally gifted in the field and at the bat. He can be counted on to advance Stanky if he has reached base, or to take matters into his own hands: He is a .300 hitter who this year leads the league in doubles.

Out there in center field is a twenty-year-old kid who started the season in Minneapolis, the Giants' Triple-A club. After thirty-five games there, in which he batted .477, the Giants couldn't keep him down on the farm any longer and summoned him to the Polo Grounds, where he promptly went 0-for-21. But Leo was convinced the kid would hit; and even if he didn't, his glove alone merited him a spot in the lineup. As the season progressed the young center fielder did get over his jitters at the plate and hit 20 homers. When he hangs up his spikes in 1973, he will have hit 640 more. His name? Willie Mays.

The arrival of Mays in the month of May led in turn to the Giants' most important move of the season: uprooting Bobby Thomson from his center-field turf and transplanting him to third base. Thomson is a good but not great player who had been enjoying a good but not great year until the Giants' closing charge, when he became the league's hottest hitter. At the other corner is Whitey Lockman, a reliable hitter and like Thomson a transplanted outfielder. Unlike Thomson, however, Lockman has become a first-rate infielder.

In the remaining two outfield posts we have Monte Irvin in left and Don Mueller in right. Irvin was a long-time star in the Negro Leagues who arrived at the Polo Grounds in 1949 as a thirty-year-old rookie. Though his best years may be behind him, he still had enough left to give the Giants an exceptional 1951 season, batting over .300, belting 24 homers, and driving home a league-high 121 runs. Mueller, only twenty-four years old and in his second year as a regular, is still developing as a hitter but already is nearly impossible to strike out, having whiffed only thirteen times all year long.

So there you have it, the team which has made the greatest stretch run in baseball history. But that accomplishment will be forgotten soon enough if victory eludes the Giants today.

Brooklyn is a formidable foe, having finished first in two of the last five seasons and second by a whisker in two others. On paper they seem a stronger team than the Giants, with pitching nearly as good, and hitting and defense which are vastly superior. We'll examine the Dodgers individually when they take the field; right now it's time to focus our attention on home plate, for a Dodger batter is in the box and Maglie is peering in at Westrum for the sign.

Sal gets off on the right foot, slipping a called strike three past Carl Furillo, but then he loses sight of the plate and walks Pee Wee Reese and Duke Snider on only nine pitches. Jackie Robinson lines a single past third, and Reese scores. The fans have hardly settled into their seats and already the home team is one run down and in trouble. But now The Barber regains his edge, inducing Andy Pafko to dribble one down to Thomson, who steps on third for the force. His throw to Lockman is too late for a twin killing, but no matter, for Gil Hodges pops to Thomson in foul ground and a big inning has been averted.

The Giants will send Eddie Stanky to the plate as their lead-off man; but before he steps in let me tell you a few things about the Dodgers, and you'll see why perhaps they *ought* to have run away with the pennant. At first base is Gil Hodges, a superlative fielder whose 40 circuit blows this year are second only to Ralph Kiner's 42; in a game last year he hit a record-tying four home runs. At second base is the incomparable Jackie Robinson, the trailblazer for all the black stars to follow and a remarkable player despite having to wait, like Monte Irvin, until he was well along in years to reach the majors. This year he hit .338 and established a record for second basemen by making only seven errors. The shortstop is Pee Wee Reese, the Dodger captain who started playing in Brooklyn in 1940 and shows no signs of slowing yet. And at third there is Billy Cox, a light hitter whose magic glove has no equal in his day.

Standing below us in left we see Andy Pafko, a proven slugger

Five of Don Newcombe's twenty wins this year have come at the expense of the Giants. The question today, however, is whether Dodger manager Charley Dressen burned Big Newk out in Philadelphia.

whose acquisition from the Cubs in midseason seemed to assure smooth sailing to the pennant. Thus far he has hit 30 homers. Patrolling center is the twenty-five-year-old Duke Snider, whose "off year" in 1951 still produced 29 homers and 101 RBI's. And in right is Carl Furillo, "The Reading Rifle," whose powerful throwing arm cut down twenty-four foolhardy runners, a league high.

The backstop is Rube Walker, substituting for the injured Roy Campanella, who struggled through the play-off opener but could go no further. Dodger manager Charley Dressen hopes his team will not feel the loss of Campy today, but how do you replace a man who hits .325, with 33 homers and 108 RBI's? And now we come to the mound where, ball in hand, his hulking frame bowed toward the plate, waits Don Newcombe. He has won 20 games thus far, and was Brooklyn's salvation in the final weekend against the Phils, throwing a shutout Saturday and five and two-thirds innings of scoreless relief on Sunday. He pitches today with only two days' rest, but Newk is strong—last year he pitched both ends of a doubleheader.

The big right-hander gets Stanky on a fly to Pafko in short left, Dark on a pop to Cox, and Mueller on a liner to Pafko. He will not be easy to solve today.

In the top of the second, Maglie breezes through the Brooks in order, fanning Walker along the way. Irvin opens the Giant second by grounding to Reese, but Lockman breaks the ice by singling past Hodges into right. Now the batter is Glasgow-born Bobby Thomson, "The Flying Scot," whose two-run homer in Game One of the play-off was the winning blow. He leans on a Newcombe fastball and drills it into left for a single, extending his hitting streak to fifteen straight games. But this is no time to accept congratulations: while Lockman stops at second as Pafko fetches the ball, here comes Thomson motoring head down onto Whitey's heels. Bobby imagined his hit would certainly reach the wall and that Lockman would scurry to third. He neglected, however, to confirm his theory by actually looking to left field or at the first-base coach, who was waving frantically to stop him. Bobby does spot Lockman at the last moment and tries to retrace his steps, but the "rock" cannot be covered up—Thomson is tagged out, and the budding rally goes for naught as Pafko races back to the wall to grab Mays's drive.

The skies have become, if possible, even more overcast than they were at game-time. As Furillo steps to the plate to start the third inning, the lights are turned on; it is only 2:04 in the afternoon. Again, Maglie puts the Dodgers down in order, this time whiffing Snider. In the bottom of the frame, with Westrum on first after a walk, Stanky smashes one down the third-base line only to have Cox intercept it and send it round the horn for a brilliant double play. In the years to follow, only Brooks Robinson and Clete Boyer will bear comparison to Cox for artistry at the hot corner.

The fourth frame is "nothing across" for both sides, but in the fifth Maglie's streak of fourteen consecutive outs is broken by Cox's leadoff bunt single. The next three Dodgers, however, flail helplessly at Sal's curves. We are only at the halfway point in the contest, yet that run Brooklyn pushed across in the first before The Barber found his form is looking bigger all the time.

After Reese throws out Lockman in the Giants' half of the fifth, Thomson hits another screamer to left, this one a surefire double since no teammate occupies second base. Newk bears down and strikes out the overanxious Mays. Now Dressen employs a mildly unorthodox strategy—with Maglie on deck, he orders an intentional walk to Westrum, the potential lead run. Dressen is fully aware that in the Polo Grounds everyone is a home-run threat, but chalks up the move as a good one when Maglie rolls out to short.

In the top of the sixth with one down, Snider, a dead-pull hitter with a picturesque swing, is fooled by a change of pace, takes a halfhearted poke at it, and dumps the ball into left off the end of his bat. With Robinson at the plate, Snider takes off for second, surprising everyone in the ball park except the Giants. Westrum calls for a pitchout, and The Duke is out by a mile. Though Robinson draws a walk, another zero goes up on the scoreboard for Brooklyn. New York fares no better in its at bats, as Cox robs Dark of a hit, and the score holds at a nerve-wracking 1–0.

Despite a two-out single by Rube Walker, the Dodgers once again shoot a blank in the seventh. Now the home-team rooters stand for the seventh-inning stretch, and this display of allegiance seems to do some good as Monte Irvin smashes a double off the left-field wall. The situation demands a sacrifice, and Lockman dumps a bunt out toward the mound—he had meant for it to roll toward third. Walker pounces on it and throws to Cox, but too late to tag the sliding Irvin. Now Giants stand on first and third with nary an out. While Newcombe paws the mound, Cox sneaks up behind Irvin trying to pull the old hidden-ball trick; Monte doesn't fall for it—he sticks to the bag. Dressen orders his infielders to play back for the double play, conceding the tying run but hoping to get out of the inning no worse than even. After fouling off two two-strike pitches, Thomson renders the maneuvering pointless as he skies to deep center, easily scoring Irvin. Newk again must face Mays in the clutch, and again he proves the master, getting Willie to smack a hard grounder to Reese for a rally-killing double play.

One to one. Now the entire season, 156 games plus, is compressed into six outs per side. There have been league play-offs in the past—in 1908 and 1946 in the National League, in 1948 in the American—but in none of these was the issue deadlocked so near to the end. Through seven innings, each hurler has permitted only four hits; if we had to guess which one might tire first, the choice would be Newcombe. A fastball pitcher who ordinarily strikes out five or six men a game, Big Newk has fanned only one to this point. Maybe the strain of last weekend's exploits is showing up after all. The Barber, on the other hand, has fanned six with his razor-sharp curveball, and has been in complete command since the first.

Furillo begins the eighth by lining one back to the box which Maglie is fortunate to stab for the out. Now, all of a sudden, both his luck and his skill run out. Reese laces a single to right and dashes to third as Snider drives a hit past Stanky's outstretched glove. With everyone on the edge of his seat, wondering if Maglie will retire Robinson or Robinson will retire Maglie, this marvelous game takes an unexpected and disappointing turn: The Barber heaves a wild pitch. Reese scoots across the plate with the lead run and Snider makes it all the way to third.

Pitching carefully to Robinson, Maglie runs the count to 3–1, then puts him on intentionally to set up a possible double play, as Dressen had done an inning earlier. Durocher looks awfully smart when Pafko smacks a hot shot to third; but the ball kicks off Thomson's glove for a tainted hit, scoring Snider and moving Robby to second. Now Hodges pops to Thomson, and there are two outs. The light-hitting Billy Cox, however, hits a wicked smash off Thomson's chest; the ball bounds away for a hit, and Robinson tallies the third run of the frame. With two men still on base, Maglie at last gets out of the inning as Walker grounds to second.

You can sense the dejection of the Giants and their fans as the players come in from the field—to have come from so far back, and to have forced the Dodgers beyond the season's end, only to lose on a wild pitch and some ground balls that should have been outs . . . it just doesn't seem right. But right or not, defeat seems a certainty as the Giants bat against Newcombe in the eighth. Newk, who relaxed his grip on the Giants' throats in

Edwin Donald Snider, the Duke of Flatbush, is only twenty-five years old and still maturing as a ballplayer. In the mid-1950s he will wallop 40 or more home runs in five consecutive seasons, a National League record.

the seventh, tightens it once more. Bill Rigney, batting for Westrum, strikes out on three pitches. Hank Thompson, hitting for Maglie, raps one to Hodges's right, which Gil gracefully backhands and flips to Newcombe, covering first. Stanky fouls out to Reese near the field boxes behind third. So much for our "educated" guess about which pitcher figured to tire first.

Coming in from the bullpen to hurl the ninth for New York is Larry Jansen, who with 22 wins this season trails Maglie by only one for league honors. The thirty-one-year-old right-hander will be working with Ray Noble, who replaces Westrum as the backstop. The Dodgers, perhaps already looking ahead to tomorrow's World Series opener, go down meekly on two grounders and a lazy fly to center.

In the dugout, Newcombe tells Dressen he's running out of gas; Dressen sends him out to the mound but alerts the bullpen to get some arms ready. Three outs are all that stand between the Dodgers and an incredibly hard-earned flag. First up for the Giants is Alvin Dark, hitless in his first three trips. Newcombe rears back and throws the best smoke he's got left, jamming him up and in, but Alvin steps off the plate and, with a protective, awkward swing, loops a single to right. Next up is left-handed Don Mueller, like Dark, hitless today.

What's this? Hodges has moved in a step or two behind Dark, obviously to hold down the size of his lead. But why? With the Giants down three, Dark is no threat to steal, and his run means nothing; by moving Hodges in behind the bag, Dressen has opened up the entire right side of the infield for Mueller. And Don, nicknamed "Mandrake the Magician" because he uses his bat like a magic wand to "hit it where they ain't," does just that. He drives a grounder to precisely the spot where Hodges would have stood had he been permitted to ignore Dark. Gil dives, but the ball bounces by, perhaps two feet beyond his reach. If Dressen had not pulled a boner, the Dodgers would have had a cinch double play, for Mueller runs poorly.

In the third-base coach's box, manager Durocher is praying that Irvin can get another single so he can have Lockman bunt the tying runs into scoring position. But Irvin lifts a pop to Hodges, and now Whitey must swing away. As he prepares for Newk's first delivery, Lockman thinks to himself that he must at all costs get the ball into the air and stay out of a possible game-ending double play. And more than get it in the air, he will try to park it in the seats. Though he connected for only 12 homers during the season, the dimensions of this park make everyone a potential Babe Ruth. Newcombe recognizes the danger and offers up a high, outside ball. For Whitey, who ordinarily is the type of hitter who goes with the pitch, thoughts of home-run glory vanish and instinct takes over. He strokes the pitch down the left-field line for a double, scoring Dark and moving Mueller to third.

Don, however, didn't begin his slide until he was almost at the bag, and now is writhing on the ground with a severely sprained ankle. While Don lies at third, surrounded by team-mates and waiting for a stretcher to be brought out, Dressen is on the phone to his bullpen coach, Clyde Sukeforth. Carl Erskine and Ralph Branca have been warming up; now Sukeforth tells him that while Erskine's got nothing, Branca's fastball looks good. So as Newcombe walks off the mound to scattered cheers and Mueller is carried out to the clubhouse in deepest center field, in comes Clint Hartung to run for Mueller and Ralph Branca to pitch for Brooklyn.

Branca, a twenty-five-year-old right-hander, was the loser in the opening game of the play-off. He had also been the loser in the opening game of the 1946 play-off. In 1947, at the age of twenty-one, he won 21 games for Brooklyn. This year he has been effective both as a starter and as a reliever: he has won 13, the same number he wears on his uniform.

Ralph Branca shows what he thinks of Lady Luck; Lady Luck will show Ralph a thing or two as well. This year he was victorious in thirteen games, one more than he will win in the next four years combined.

The batter is Bobby Thomson, who last inning made the Giant faithful wish that Billy Cox had been playing third for *their* side. On the other hand, he has gone 4-for-9 thus far in the play-off and did drive in the tying run in the seventh. While Branca tosses in his warm-ups, Durocher confers with Thomson. What he says, we will learn later, is, "Bobby, if you ever hit one, hit one now!"

The thought crosses Dressen's mind whether, with men on second and third, to walk the dangerous Thomson intentionally and pitch to Mays, the overanxious rookie who has been a flop at the plate this afternoon. Charley had employed this strategy successfully, though with far less risk, in the fifth. But this time he decides to go with the book and does not put the potential winning run on base.

Assuming his stance in the batter's box, Thomson remembers that the pitch he hit off Branca for the game-winning homer two days ago was a waist-high fastball, so that's the one pitch he *knows* he won't see now. But surprise, surprise, that is precisely what Branca fires in, and Thomson takes it for a strike. Lockman, perched on second, thinks, "Oh, no, he'll never get another pitch like that again."

And he's right. The next pitch is a fastball high and inside, the kind pitchers had been getting him out on all season long. It is not a strike but a "purpose pitch" designed to set Thomson up for a curveball away on the next pitch. But Bobby takes a cut at it, meets it squarely, and the ball sails out in a low arc toward us in left. Here comes Andy Pafko, racing to the wall at the 315-foot mark and hoping the liner will start to drop. On the mound, Branca whirls to follow the flight of the ball, muttering, "Sink, sink, *sink!*" Thomson runs head down to first at full speed, for though he knows he has hit the ball hard, he doesn't think it will reach the stands. As he nears first he looks up, in time to see his drive sink, sink, sink—not into Pafko's waiting glove, but barely over the wall of the lower left-field stands! The Giants win!

The shot heard 'round the world . . . baseball has seen many heroic home runs, but never one quite like this.

A tremendous roar fills the old stadium, which has never seen a finish like this one. The Giants and their fans are jumping up and down, hugging each other in disbelief, shouting, laughing, crying from joy. Had there ever been a season such as this, a game the equal of this one? It is the Miracle of Coogan's Bluff. The Dodgers and their faithful stand silent and hollow, trying to absorb the enormity of what has just happened. With one swing of the bat, the game that was won is lost. The pennant that was theirs now belongs to the hated Giants. The campaign that was to reach its climax in the World Series is now over. A thirteen-and-a-half game lead in mid-August, and now . . . nothing.

As Thomson realizes that the ball is in the seats, he begins to hop, then skip, then trot around the bases, the picture of joy unbounded. At home plate he is swallowed up in the throng of teammates and fans waiting to share this moment with him. It's a great moment for Thomson, for the Giants, for baseball—but cast your eyes toward the outfield, where a scattered procession of somber Dodgers paces off the interminably long trip to the center-field clubhouse. Walking by himself, feeling the complete weight of the Dodger collapse on his shoulders, is Ralph Branca —Number 13—who forever after will be remembered as the "goat" of this incredible game, just as Bobby Thomson, very nearly the goat himself, will be remembered as its hero. One pitch, one swing—a goat, a hero—and the 156 games that have gone before, and the countless opportunities for victory along the way, are all forgotten. It's unreasonable, and it's cruel, but there's no changing it now.

October 3, 1951

BROOKLYN	AB	R	H	P	A	E
Furillo, rf.	5	0	0	0	0	0
Reese, ss.	4	2	1	2	5	0
Snider, cf.	3	1	2	1	0	0
Robinson, 2b.	2	1	1	3	2	0
Pafko, lf.	4	0	1	4	1	0
Hodges, 1b.	4	0	0	11	1	0
Cox, 3b.	4	0	2	1	3	0
Walker, c.	4	0	1	2	0	0
Newcombe, p.	4	0	0	1	1	0
Branca, p.	0	0	0	0	0	0
TOTALS	34	4	8	25	13	0

NEW YORK	AB	R	H	P	A	E
Stanky, 2b.	4	0	0	0	4	0
Dark, ss.	4	1	1	2	2	0
Mueller, rf.	4	0	1	0	0	0
c Hartung	0	1	0	0	0	0
Irvin, lf.	4	1	1	1	0	0
Lockman, 1b.	3	1	2	11	1	0
*Thomson, 3b.	4	1	3	4	1	0
Mays, cf.	3	0	0	1	0	0
Westrum, c.	0	0	0	7	1	0
a Rigney	1	0	0	0	0	0
Noble, c.	0	0	0	0	0	0
Maglie, p.	2	0	0	1	2	0
b Thompson	1	0	0	0	0	0
Jansen, p.	0	0	0	0	0	0
TOTALS	30	5	8	27	11	0

a Struck out for Westrum in 8th
b Grounded out for Maglic in 8th
c Ran for Mueller in 9th
* Charged with AB for Sac. Fly in accordance with scoring rules of 1951

```
BROOKLYN    100  000  030 — 4
NEW YORK    000  000  104 — 5
```

RBI—Robinson, Thomson 4, Pafko, Cox, Lockman. 2B—Thomson, Irvin, Lockman. HR—Thomson. CS—Snider. Sac.—Lockman. DP—Bkn. 2. LOB—Bkn. 7, N.Y. 3. Umpires—Jorda, Conlan, Stewart, Goetz. Time—2:28. Att.—34,320.

BROOKLYN	IP	H	R	ER	BB	SO
Newcombe	8⅓	7	4	4	2	2
**Branca (L)	0	1	1	1	0	0
NEW YORK						
Maglie	8	8	4	4	4	6
Jansen (W)	1	0	0	0	0	0

**Pitched to one batter in 9th
WP—Maglie

October 8, 1956
Brooklyn Dodgers
vs.
New York Yankees

How do you top a game like that one? You don't; but come with me from the Polo Grounds in Manhattan, across the Harlem River, to Yankee Stadium in the Bronx. A classic World Series pitching duel awaits us there, and I guarantee you won't be disappointed.

It is five years since "the shot heard 'round the world." Bobby Thomson has just concluded a miserable season with Milwaukee; Ralph Branca is washed up at the age of thirty; managers Durocher and Dressen have both been dumped; and the Giants are a sixth-place club. But the Dodgers, sporting much the same lineup we saw on that fateful day in 1951, have topped the National League for the fourth time in the last five years. In fact, if only they could have changed the results of the final day of the regular season in 1951, 1950, and 1946, they might have captured nine flags in eleven seasons.

That performance would have put them on a par with their opponents this afternoon—almost; for the Bronx Bombers, who have taken nine of the last ten American League titles, had also won the World Series their last seven tries before 1955. What happened that year? Brooklyn beat them. In short, we're going to be looking at two awfully good baseball clubs, the best this decade has to offer and among the best of all time.

The Yankee Stadium we are entering is "the house that Ruth built" back in 1923, not the park of the 1980s, modernized at an expense of some hundred million dollars. The triple-tiered original, with its wedding-cake masonry and broad expanse of outfield green, has come to be almost a national ball park, for it seems the World Series, America's autumn celebration, is played here every year. It is a beautiful place to watch a game, and I've secured two dandy seats behind home. We'll have more than 64,000 fans for company. Though it is a perfect afternoon, with the nip of fall softened by the radiant sun, keep that jacket on— there'll be no sun where we sit.

The dimensions here are eccentric, like those of most of the old parks, and favor left-handed hitters with power (Ruth and Gehrig in days gone by, Berra and Mantle today). Though the measurements to the foul lines are similar—296 to right and 301 to left—the wall in right tapers out modestly to 367 feet, while in left the wall is a distant 415 feet from home. In center field, where monuments to Yankee greats are placed near the warning track, a ball may travel 465 feet and yet fall short of the wall.

The four games played prior to today's have been split, with the Brooks taking the first two right here, and the Yanks fighting back to take the next two at Ebbets Field. In the Dodger victories, the batting hero was Gil Hodges, who in the two games drove home seven runs, and the pitching star was—Giant fans cannot believe it—Sal Maglie, who tossed a complete game to win the opener. The Barber, now thirty-nine years old, had been sent packing by the Giants in 1955 and was picked up by the Dodgers shortly after the '56 campaign began. Though everyone else thought Sal was over the hill, he rewarded the Dodgers' faith in him by going 13–5, including a no-hitter less than two weeks ago. Manager Walter Alston has named him to hurl today.

The Yankee skipper, Casey Stengel, will give the ball to Don Larsen, a twenty-seven-year-old right-hander who only two years ago posted an atrocious mark of 3–21 with Baltimore. Entrusted with a 6–0 lead as the starter in Game Two of this Series, Larsen failed to get past the second inning. So why is Casey placing his bet on Don again in this pivotal contest? Because in September, which opened with Larsen's record standing at only 7–5, Stengel began to see signs that Larsen was becoming a pitcher rather than a thrower; was learning how to harness the natural ability that everyone in baseball knew he had in him.

The month started with two low-hit wins which jacked up Larsen's confidence, and then a change in his delivery on September 20 seemed to work wonders for his control. Facing the Boston Red Sox that day, Larsen decided to pitch the entire game without using a windup—pitching as if he had a man on base at all times, which in the not too distant past had seemed close to the truth. The reason for this experiment was solely to foil Boston's third-base coach, Del Baker, who Don suspected was stealing his pitches and tipping the Boston batters. After the game, which he won 2–1, Don was delighted with his innovation. "I fooled the batters better," he said. "I had better control, and I fooled Baker. It's wonderful."

Don Larsen

The new motion required plenty of arm strength to throw hard for nine innings, but at 6′4″ and 215 pounds, Don had strength to spare. Control had been his problem. Though his poor showing in Game Two was the result of four walks in his one and two-thirds innings, Stengel chalked that up to nervousness induced by the short fences of Ebbets Field. He is counting on Larsen to fare better in Yankee Stadium, where a fleet center fielder can erase many a pitcher's mistake.

And in center field the Yankees boast the fleetest of the fleet, and the strongest of the strong—the best player in baseball this year, Mickey Mantle. Only twenty-four years old, he hit .353, belted 52 homers, and drove in 130 runs—all league highs, thus giving him the Triple Crown. This feat has been accomplished only ten times before in major-league history, and will be only two times more in future years. He has proven himself a worthy successor to Joe DiMaggio both at the plate and in the field, where his lightning speed enables him to outrun balls hit in the canyons of Yankee Stadium's vast center field.

Mickey's getting ready for the start of the game, playing catch with left-fielder Enos Slaughter, who was playing major-league baseball when Mickey was in the second grade. Forty years old, "Country" Slaughter was picked up by New York in August to aid in the pennant drive. Thus far he has been the Yanks' top hitter in the Series. Across the outfield in right is Hank Bauer, a thirty-four-year-old veteran coming off a strange year in which he posted his worst batting average and best home-run and RBI totals. Yesterday he hit a big four-bagger in the Yankee win.

The Yankee infield is dependable, if not star-studded. At third is Andy Carey, an unaccomplished hitter but fine gloveman. The shortstop is Gil McDougald, moved over from the keystone this year when Phil Rizzuto, at age thirty-seven, finally wore out. Gil enjoyed his best year at the plate, hitting .311. At second, reclaiming his spot after nearly two years of military service, is Billy Martin, a scrapper in the tradition of Harris and Stanky and a tremendous Series performer. And at first is platoon-player Joe Collins who, unlike fellow first-baseman Moose Skowron, bats from the left side of the plate and thus is in the lineup against Maglie today.

Behind the plate is Yogi Berra. Through hard work, this stubby, awkward-looking performer has made himself into the best catcher in the American League, as valuable in the field as he is at the bat. His contributions to the club through the years have been recognized with three Most Valuable Player Awards. No man has ever won more, and with 30 homers and 105 RBI's this year Yogi might have gotten his fourth but for Mantle.

Yogi fires Larsen's final pregame pitch back to him, and we are under way. Stepping in for the Dodgers is Jim "Junior" Gilliam, a .300 hitter who several years ago moved a slowing Jackie Robinson off second base. With the count 2–2, Larsen slips a pitch over the edge of the plate that Gilliam disdains. Umpire Babe Pinelli, behind the plate for the last time after twenty-two years in blue, calls it strike three. Shortstop Pee Wee Reese, now thirty-eight and fading, fouls off a pitch for a strike, then works the count to 3–2. (Make a note of that on your scorecard, for Larsen will not go to three balls on another batter today!) Then Reese also takes a called strike three. Next up is Duke Snider, the National League home-run leader with 43 this year. The Duke runs the count to 2–1 before hitting a Larsen slider on a line to Bauer in right.

The Dodger strategy in the first seemed to be to wait Larsen out and see if he'd walk himself into trouble, as he did in Game Two. The three Brooklyn batters forced Don to throw fifteen pitches to retire the side; but now they are convinced of his control, and Don will not throw more pitches than that in any inning to follow.

The Dodgers take the field behind Maglie. As in 1951, Hodges is at first, Reese at shortstop, Snider in center, Furillo in right, and Campanella behind the plate. Robinson has switched from second base to third, replacing Billy Cox, now retired. The only newcomer besides Gilliam is left-fielder Sandy Amoros, a diminutive twenty-six-year-old from Havana who surprised the Dodgers with sixteen homers as a part-timer. In the field he is best described as erratic, capable of making the tough play but blowing the routine one. His splendid catch in the final game of the Series last year was vital to the Dodgers' victory. And Maglie, of course, is a newcomer, too. He retires the Yankees in order, Bauer popping to short, Collins bunting too hard to third and being thrown out, and Mantle flying to left.

Leading off the second for Brooklyn is Jackie Robinson, a graying and paunchy thirty-seven. This coming winter he will suffer the indignity of being traded to the Giants, and will retire rather than report. But back to the game at hand: Jackie takes a strike, then smashes a liner toward the hole in left. Carey stabs at the hard-hit shot but cannot hold it in his glove; it deflects to shortstop Gil McDougald, who picks the ball up on one bounce and rifles it to first, nipping Robby by a half stride. After Hodges fans, Amoros, on a 2–2 pitch, pops the ball into shallow right. Martin backpedals on the ball, an ordinary play, but misjudges the flight and must reach back over his head to make the catch; in doing so he topples onto his back, but holds the ball. The Yankees also go down one, two, three to The Barber, and we move on to the third.

The third inning is, if possible, less eventful than the two that preceded it. Eighteen men up, eighteen men down. The pattern reminds us of that game we saw in Chicago back in 1917, though of course this contest is still too young to compare the two. As you know, a pitchers' duel is exciting in a different way from the "ordinary" game—the very absence of action which makes the game so humdrum in the early innings, if continued into the late going, *becomes* the action. Though watching a slugfest is more fun, the excitement of a game that is beautifully pitched by both men is doubled: We lean forward in our seats, nervous not only about which team will win, but also about which pitcher will have his work of art crowned with glory and which will have his tarnished in defeat.

In the fourth, Larsen's first two pitches produce fast outs: Gilliam grounds to Martin, as does Reese, trying to check his swing. Next up is Snider, who at this point has hit more World Series home runs in his career than anyone except Babe Ruth or Lou Gehrig. In a scoreless duel, he is one guy you have to be very careful with, and Larsen is. His first pitch is off the plate, and so is his second. This is the first time he has been behind a batter 2–0 (mark that on your scorecard, too). The left-handed slugger with the peculiar stance tenses his body into readiness, brings his forearms up parallel with the ground, and cocks his bat in expectation of a fastball down the middle. He does get a fat pitch, but it is a slider rather than a fastball; out in front of the fractionally slower pitch, Duke pulls one down the line, in the lower rightfield seats for sure. But it is foul. The crowd roars its pleasure and Larsen goes on to fan the mighty Duke of Flatbush for his fifth strikeout in four innings.

Maglie keeps mowing the Yankees down in the bottom of the fourth as Bauer grounds to third and Collins goes down on strikes. But then the break comes. Mantle leans on a Maglie curveball and sends it down the line in right, the same path that Snider's hit followed in the top of the frame; but Mantle's drive wraps around the foul pole for a home run! There'll be no double no-hit game this day. The heretofore silent crowd erupts into cheers as their golden boy rounds the bases with his third home run of the Series, one short of the record shared by Ruth . . . and Snider. Berra follows with another hard-hit ball, a liner to center; The Duke races in, dives, and comes up with a shoestring catch.

Armed with that tissue-thin lead, Larsen gets Robinson on a fairly deep fly to right to commence the fifth. The batter to follow is Gil Hodges, whose "off year" in '56 still produced 32 homers and 87 RBI's. Big Don goes up 0–2 in the count, then throws two wide-sweeping breaking pitches, Gil's notorious weakness. But Gil, though tempted, watches them go by. Now Larsen must come back over the plate and—crack! The ball soars into left-center field, a sure double, perhaps a triple, even for the slow-footed Hodges. Wait—here comes Mantle racing over to cut off the alley. Bending as he takes his final stride, he extends his glove hand and plucks the ball out of the air, a sensational play. Already rocked for two long clouts in the inning, Larsen gives up another, this time to Sandy Amoros, but it lands foul among the fans in the lower right-field stands. Sandy goes on to ground out to Martin.

In the Yankee fifth Slaughter draws the first walk of the game, but is erased on Martin's force-out. Billy in turn is erased as Reese takes McDougald's liner and fires to first before Billy can return. But after Larsen once again sets the Brooks down in order in the top of the sixth, the Yankees mount a rally. Carey singles and Larsen, despite having two strikes on him, risks the

Mickey Mantle makes the defensive play of the game in left-center field, robbing Gil Hodges of an extra-base hit. Though not blessed with the great instinct and judgment of a DiMaggio, Mantle is a first-rate center fielder.

strikeout and bunts in front of the plate; Campanella's only play is to first. Now Bauer singles into left. Amoros, coming in fast, appears to have a play at home on Carey—but the ball rolls up his arm as he tries to glove it, and Carey crosses the plate standing up. It's 2–0.

The batter now, Joe Collins, is the big out of the inning, the man Maglie must retire to keep the game within reach, for following Collins is Mantle. But Joe, a thirty-three-year-old journeyman who this year hit only .225, belts an inside fastball to right center for a single. Bauer makes third, and Yankee fans are ecstatic. Their Bronx Bombers are about to blow this game wide open.

Or so they think. After a visit to the mound by Walter Alston, designed mostly to stall for time to get his bullpen active, Maglie works Mantle down and in and gets him to ground to Hodges. Gil has Bauer trapped off third, but coolly steps on first to retire Mantle, *then* throws to Campy, who starts the rundown between third and home. Bauer dances back and forth for all he's worth, and the Dodgers nearly botch the play. Campy's low throw sends Robinson sprawling into the dirt to make the catch, but at last Jackie makes the tag. The Dodgers are still within reach: When (shall we say if?) they get a man on, they can tie things up with one swing.

A haze has been slowly settling over the stadium, and the shadows have been lengthening from where we sit out toward home plate and then the mound, making the hitters' task even harder, if that is possible today. Larsen just keeps flipping that ball to Berra, nice and easy, as if he were pitching batting practice. That no-windup style is certainly deceptive. Though he's had good hard stuff when he's wanted to show it, the key to his performance thus far today has been, first, his impeccable control, and second, his ability to keep the Dodgers off balance by changing speeds. The only pitch that has been hittable is Larsen's slider, which has been responsible for most of the close calls he's had.

There are no close calls for Larsen in the seventh, though McDougald is called upon to make a nice pickup of Gilliam's short-hop smash for the first out of the inning. Reese hits the ball deep to center, but on a high arc; Mantle glides under it. Then Snider lifts an easy fly to Slaughter, and the unspoken drama continues.

In the Yankees' turn at bat, Maglie takes care of Berra and Slaughter, then allows a minor uprising—single to Martin, walk to McDougald—before disposing of Carey. Few in this crowd are interested in the bottom halves of innings anymore, except to get them out of the way as quickly as possible. The buzz of the crowd, constant in any World Series game, has intensified with each passing frame; the buzz became a hum, the hum became a drone, and the drone is fast advancing upon a roar. Everyone can see the scoreboard with its line of goose eggs after "Brooklyn," and some may be so bold as to violate the ancient baseball taboo against mentioning a no-hitter in progress. There—I've done it, too; the drama is no longer unspoken, so I may as well say a few words more on the subject.

No one has ever thrown a no-hitter in the World Series. Three men have thrown one-hitters (and another will in the years to follow), but only one man has taken a no-hitter into the ninth inning: Bill Bevens of the Yankees, who recorded all but the final out in Game Four of the 1947 Series without allowing a hit, then on one pitch lost his no-hitter and the ball game. Bevens's game was marred by the ten walks he allowed; Larsen, on the other hand, has walked no one. He has also not hit anyone with a pitch, nor has he been victimized by an error in the field. He has, in short, been perfect. In the entire history of major-league baseball, from 1876 to this day in 1956, only six men have pitched perfect games, and none since Charley Robertson did it in 1922. Larsen is trying to join that select fraternity, but he still has six tough outs to go. In the 1927 Series, Yankee left-hander Herb Pennock was in the same position as Don, but he could retire only one more batter before seeing his perfect game, his no-hitter, and his shutout disappear in the eighth.

Jackie Robinson is first up. He takes a called strike one, fouls off the next pitch for strike two, and hits back to Larsen, who throws to first. Now Don must contend with Hodges, who drove that ball to deep left center in the fifth. Gil runs the count to 2–2, then belts a vicious liner to the left of Carey; Andy takes a step, dips, and the ball zips into his glove for the second out. Now Don has run his flawless string out past Pennock's. Amoros drives one deep to center, but not deep enough to give Mantle a difficult play. Twenty-four men down; three to go.

The roar of the crowd continues as the teams exchange field, and mounts in an awesome crescendo as Larsen steps to the plate. Everyone rises to give this unlikely hero the ovation of his life, showering love upon him for what he has done thus far and giving encouragement for what he has yet to do. His mind understandably not on his batwork, Larsen fans. So do Bauer and Collins; Maglie is pitching quite a game, too.

Through the early innings, Larsen's lumbering physique, easy pitching motion, and blank expression have given him an air of nonchalance, as if he were pitching a softball game at the company picnic. But now, as he stands on the mound waiting for Carl Furillo to get set in the batter's box, he feels "so weak in the knees I thought I was going to faint," he will say later. The 64,519 paying customers feel the same way.

Here we go. Furillo swings at the first pitch and fouls it off. He swings at the next pitch, and fouls *it* off. After taking a ball, he fouls one into the first-base boxes and another into the boxes in right. Larsen still has his stuff, or Furillo wouldn't be hitting everything to the opposite field. The fifth pitch to Furillo produces a fly to medium right, a piece of cake for Bauer. *One down.*

Now for Roy Campanella, like Yogi Berra a three-time MVP, but this year suffering from a bad hand that cost him 99 points off his previous year's batting average. He may not be the Campy of old, but he's still dangerous, as Larsen finds out with his first pitch. Campy crunches a fastball to deep left that Larsen instantly thinks is a home run. But at the last second the ball hooks foul, and Roy bounces the next pitch down to Martin for an easy out. *Two down.*

The scheduled batter is the ninth man in the order, as it must be when you get to within one out of a perfect game. Will Alston let Maglie bat for himself and make it easy for Larsen? Not on your life; remember, the Dodgers are still only two runs from a tie. Coming to the plate is Dale Mitchell, a late-season pickup from the Indians who is thirty-five years old and a .312 hitter for his career. Veteran sportswriters in the press box may be thinking back to a game in August of 1932, when Detroit's Tommy Bridges, one out short of a perfect game, was touched for a single by Washington pinch-hitter Dave Harris.

Larsen turns his back to home plate and looks out over the stadium, thinking his private thoughts. (Later he will reveal that he was saying to himself, "Please, help me, somebody.") As Mitchell, a left-handed batter, steps in, Don turns and takes his sign. The first pitch is a fastball, off the plate, and the stadium groans. Next Yogi calls for a slider; Mitchell declines to offer, but Pinelli calls a strike. Now back to the fastball. Mitchell swings—and misses. This is it: One more strike and the impossible will be made real. Larsen fires another fastball; Mitchell swings, and the fans gasp as contact is made . . . but the ball drifts foul off to the left. Larsen reloads the rifle, says to himself, "Here goes nothing," and fires another bullet toward the outside edge of the plate. Mitchell keeps his bat on his shoulder. Pinelli raises his arm. It's a strike! The game is over!

The scoreboard tells it all. Number 8 is Dale Mitchell, who is about to strike out on Don Larsen's ninety-seventh pitch of the game. The second baseman is a fellow named Billy Martin.

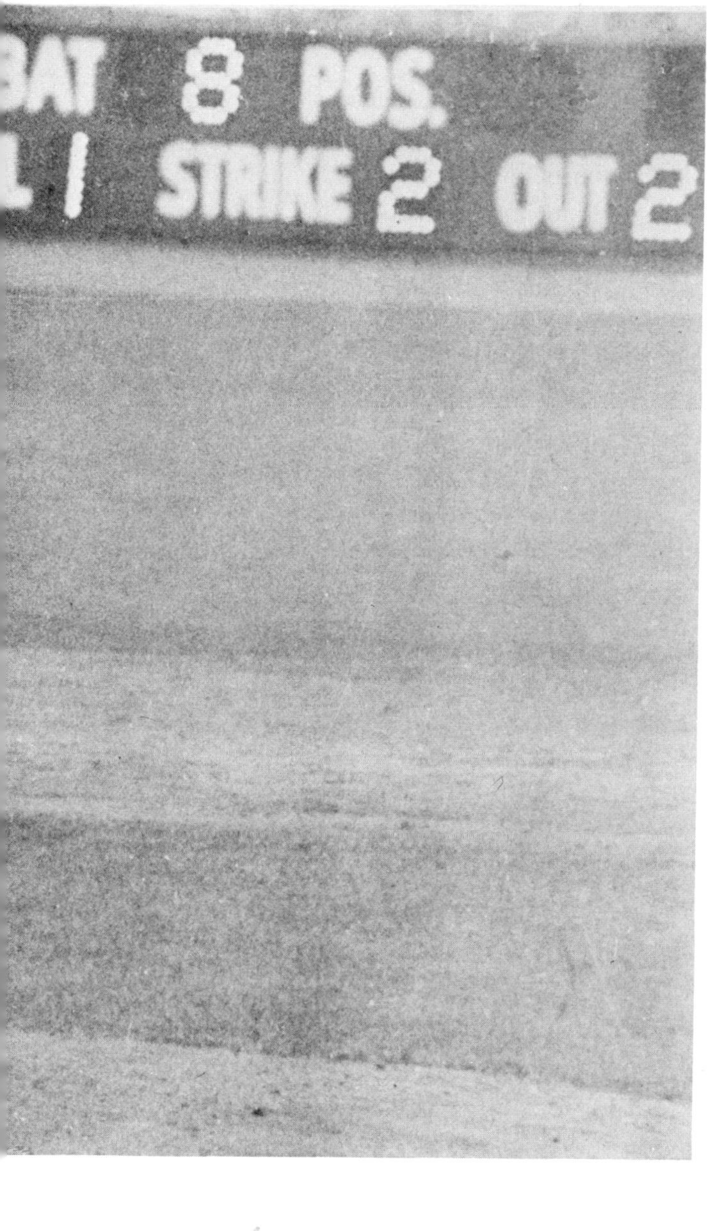
BAT 8 POS.
L 1 STRIKE 2 OUT 2

Yogi rushes out from the plate and leaps on Larsen in a total bear hug. Mitchell jaws at Pinelli in futility while Yankee players and fans swarm onto the field to pound and pummel the man who made the magic. Fate has plucked Don Larsen from the ranks today and has set him upon a pedestal above all the heroes of the past; in baseball's grandest arena, in its most storied setting, he has tasted immortality. He is the perfect one.

October 8, 1956

BROOKLYN

	AB	R	H	P	A	E
Gilliam, 2b.	3	0	0	2	0	0
Reese, ss.	3	0	0	4	2	0
Snider, cf.	3	0	0	1	0	0
Robinson, 3b.	3	0	0	2	4	0
Hodges, 1b.	3	0	0	5	1	0
Amoros, lf.	3	0	0	3	0	0
Furillo, rf.	3	0	0	0	0	0
Campanella, c. ...	3	0	0	7	2	0
Maglie, p.	2	0	0	0	1	0
*Mitchell	1	0	0	0	0	0
TOTALS	27	0	0	24	10	0

NEW YORK

	AB	R	H	P	A	E
Bauer, rf.	4	0	1	4	0	0
Collins, 1b.	4	0	1	7	0	0
Mantle, cf.	3	1	1	4	0	0
Berra, c.	3	0	0	7	0	0
Slaughter, lf.	2	0	0	1	0	0
Martin, 2b.	3	0	1	3	4	0
McDougald, ss.	2	0	0	0	2	0
Carey, 3b.	3	1	1	1	1	0
Larsen, p.	2	0	0	0	1	0
TOTALS	26	2	5	27	8	0

*Struck out for Maglie in 9th

BROOKLYN	000	000	000 — 0
NEW YORK	000	101	00x — 2

RBI—Mantle, Bauer. HR—Mantle. Sac.—Larsen. DP—Bkn. 2. LOB—Bkn. 0, N.Y. 3. Umpires—Pinelli, Soar, Boggess, Napp, Gorman, Runge. Time—2:06. Att.—64,519.

BROOKLYN	IP	H	R	ER	BB	SO
Maglie	8	5	2	2	2	5

NEW YORK	IP	H	R	ER	BB	SO
Larsen	9	0	0	0	0	7

May 26, 1959
Pittsburgh Pirates
vs.
Milwaukee Braves

Fate can be cruel, as it was to Ralph Branca, or kind, as it was to Don Larsen. This night it will be both to Harvey Haddix, in a game unlike any other in major-league history.

The scene is Milwaukee County Stadium, home of the defending National League champion Braves, who are leading the pack once again early in the season. Opposing them on this warm, humid evening are the Pirates of Pittsburgh, perennial cellar dwellers whose youngsters surprised everyone last year: Behind manager Danny Murtaugh, in his first full year at the helm, the Buccaneers gave the Braves a battle and finished second. Nearly 20,000 people have come out despite the overcast skies, high winds, and occasional flashes of lightning. Folks in Milwaukee love their Braves.

And who can blame them? Since the Dodgers at last grew old in 1957 and decrepit in 1958, the Braves' array of talent has become the best in the National League; it gained for them a World Series win over the Yankees in '57 and a near miss last year. With sluggers like Henry Aaron, Eddie Mathews, and Joe Adcock and pitchers like Warren Spahn, Lew Burdette, and Bob Buhl, the Braves seem in good position to follow the Dodgers as the dominant team for years to come.

Let's take seats along the third-base line and look out over the stadium as the Milwaukee players ready for the game. County Stadium is a fairly cozy place for hitters despite its nearly sym-metrical design. It's only 320 to the left-field corner, 402 to dead center, and 315 down the line in right—and most appetiz-ingly, a very reachable 362 feet to the alleys. What's more, the ball carries well. This year Eddie Mathews will hit 46 homers, Henry Aaron 39, Joe Adcock 25, and Wes Covington 21; not surprisingly, the Braves as a team will lead the majors in home runs.

These four belters are all in the lineup tonight. Aaron, in right, is only twenty-five years old, yet on his way to a second batting title; coming into tonight's game he is batting over .470. What no one suspects is that he is also on his way to hitting more career home runs than Babe Ruth. In the outfield, he covers a lot of ground and has a fine throwing arm. In left, Covington makes every play an adventure, but the Braves have no complaints about his bat. The left-handed slugger hit .330 last season and knocked in 74 runs in under 300 at bats. At the third-base corner, Mathews is the most powerful hitter ever to play the position. He moved to Milwaukee with the franchise back in 1953, and im-mediately won over the fans when, though only twenty-one, he hit 47 homers. Hard work through the years has made him better than average with the glove. And across the diamond at first is thirty-one-year-old Joe Adcock, who has hit as many as 38 homers in a season and in a game against the Dodgers in 1954 clouted four homers and a double, the all-time record for total bases.

Up the middle the Braves do not boast the same degree of strength. In center is thirty-eight-year-old Andy Pafko (remember him from 1951?). He hasn't got much left as a player, and will pack it in when this season is over. Tonight he is subbing for the Braves' regular out there, Billy Bruton. At second is Johnny O'Brien, one of seven men manager Fred Haney will use at the keystone this year in a vain attempt to replace Red Schoendienst, last year's regular who was stricken by tuberculosis. Six years ago O'Brien came up to Pittsburgh along with his twin brother, Eddie, and the pair formed the Pirate double-play combo for half a season: great idea, dreadful results. The shortstop, Johnny Logan, is one of the league's best, a scrapper who covers a lot of acreage and can be relied upon to hit .270 or so.

The backstop is Del Crandall, who, like Mathews, Logan, Adcock, and Pafko, has been in Milwaukee since the beginning. He is at this moment the best all-around catcher in the National League. And on the mound is Selva Lewis Burdette, also known as Saliva Lew for his universally suspected but not yet detected spitball. Lew has all the pitches—fastball, slider, curve, change—but like Gaylord Perry in the years to come, he fidgets around and brings his fingers toward his mouth on every pitch to make the batter *think* he's going to get the spitter. Lew has been, with Warren Spahn, the foundation of the Milwaukee pitching staff for years; in the 1957 World Series he grabbed the national spotlight by winning all three games he started, including two shutouts. As he peers in for the sign for his first delivery tonight, the thirty-two-year-old right-hander is the top winner in the league with a 7–2 mark.

One, two, three the Pirates go down, politely as you please.

Lew Burdette is so fidgety on the mound—bringing his hand to his cap, his mouth, his uniform—that his manager, Fred Haney, says of him, "Lew would make coffee nervous."

The Braves trot in for their first licks, and now we'll review the Bucs in the field.

Whipping the ball around the infield are Don Hoak at third, Dick "Ducky" Schofield at short, Bill Mazeroski at second, and Rocky Nelson at first. Hoak, a former Marine and professional prizefighter, is a tough guy who came up in the Dodger organization and was acquired this year in hopes that his winning spirit would rub off on his younger teammates. Aside from his "intangibles," Hoak is a respectable hitter and first-rate fielder. Schofield is a utility infielder giving regular shortstop Dick Groat a breather tonight. He can't hit but, incredibly, will last nineteen years in the majors. At second is Mazeroski, only twenty-two years old, yet described by many long-time observers of the game as the best with the glove they've ever seen. And he's no automatic out at the plate—last year he hit .275 and belted 19 homers. First baseman Rocky Nelson is one of the great mysteries of baseball: In the minors he has won three batting, home-run, and RBI crowns, and three times he has been named Most Valuable Player in the International League; yet each time he's called up to the big leagues he flops. This is his eighth major-league trial, and since he is thirty-four years old, it's sure to be his last if he doesn't pan out.

In left field is Bob Skinner, a line-drive-type hitter who batted .321 last year; the less said about his defense the better. But if Skinner can't scamper into left center to nab those long drives, center fielder Bill Virdon sure can. Unfortunately, he doesn't hit much. Put Virdon and Skinner together and you'd have a heck of a ballplayer—one almost as good as the man the Pirates usually have in right field, Roberto Clemente. But Roberto went on the disabled list yesterday with an injured arm, and his replacement tonight, Roman Mejias, is simply adequate.

Behind the plate is the veteran Smoky Burgess, a 5'8", 200-pound fireplug who can hit with the best of them; as a receiver he is fair. And on the mound is Harvey Haddix, a thirty-five-year-old left-hander who made a big splash as a rookie in 1953, winning twenty games with the Cards, and has been only an average starter since. A little guy who looks smaller than his listed 5′9″ and 160 pounds, Haddix can muster a surprisingly zippy fastball to go with his assortment of breaking pitches.

Called "The Kitten" for his resemblance to Harry "The Cat" Brecheen, another little left-hander who was with the Cards when Haddix broke in, he has been fighting off a cold the last few days. As soon as the Pirates arrived in Milwaukee this afternoon, Harvey went to his hotel room and got into bed—and if tonight were not his turn to pitch, that's where he would have stayed. But here he is, sucking a throat lozenge while throwing his warm-ups, thinking to himself that his stuff looks as lousy as he feels. Somehow he escapes the first inning without getting roughed up, as O'Brien grounds to short, Mathews lines one straight at Nelson, and Aaron lifts a fly to Virdon.

Nelson opens the Pirate second with a single to right, but is snuffed out as Skinner grounds to Adcock, who starts a 3–6–3 double play, first to short and back to first. Burdette gets Mazeroski on one of his special "sinkers," and it's the Braves' turn. Haddix fans the dangerous Adcock, and gets Covington and Crandall on easy groundouts. Not a whole lot of excitement yet, I know, but don't go in search of a hot dog, not just yet.

Don Hoak smacks a single to left to get things going in the third, but is forced out by Mejias. Next up is Haddix, a good hitter for a pitcher who has on occasion been used as a pinch hitter. He raps a liner back to the box, off Burdette's leg and out toward second base. Mejias, in a bit of risky base running, roars past second base without hesitation and dashes for third. If he makes it, Roman's gamble will be applauded as daring and bold; if he doesn't, it's a bonehead play. Johnny Logan hustles over from shortstop, scoops up the ball, wheels, and fires a strike to

Nicknamed "Tiger," Don Hoak is another in the long line of players valued more for their drive to win than for any particular ability. Bucky Harris, Eddie Stanky, Billy Martin—these are Hoak's kindred spirits.

Mathews at third. Mejias is out by a healthy margin. The base-running blunder looks even worse when Ducky Schofield follows with a single to right that sends Haddix to third; the Pirates could now be on the scoreboard. Virdon flies out to end the rally, and the run that did not score will loom large.

Haddix sets the side down in order in the third, the fourth, and the fifth, baffling the Braves with his array of pitches. He is relying mostly on the fastball and slider, yet has recorded outs with his off-speed curve, screwball, and straight change as well. Burdette, meanwhile, allows a single to Skinner in the fourth and another to Mejias in the fifth but, aided by a double play, holds up his end of the emerging pitching duel. In the next three innings, Lew will be even sharper, retiring all nine Pirates to face him; his only scare will come in the seventh, when Skinner's high drive to right will appear to be a home run, then be swept back onto the playing field by the gusting winds that have swirled about the stadium through much of this game.

Haddix opens the sixth by pulling the string on his fastball and getting Pafko to pop to Nelson. The next batter is Logan, who in the third inning came closest of the Braves to registering a hit when Schofield had to leap to grab his line drive. This time Johnny tests the Pittsburgh shortstop again, knocking a grounder into the hole; Schofield glides to his right, backhands the ball, plants his back foot, and makes the long throw across the diamond just in time. Burdette whiffs, and Haddix enters upon the final third of the game, the point at which people begin to think in terms of a no-hitter. Actually, Harvey has been aware of the goose egg in the Braves' hit column on the scoreboard since the third inning; what he doesn't realize is that he's also working on a perfect game.

As Haddix heads to the mound for the bottom of the seventh, the rain which has been threatening for hours finally starts to come—not a cloudburst, but an unpleasant drizzle which sends some of the fans scurrying for cover. Haddix continues his progress toward every pitcher's dream by getting O'Brien and Aaron on bouncers to third and fanning Mathews. And the eighth proves equally routine, with Adcock whiffing for the second time, Covington lofting a fly to left, and Crandall grounding to Hoak.

Now we go to the ninth. There have been five hits in the game, all belonging to Pittsburgh, but Burdette has been no less immaculate than Haddix over the last three innings. The Pirates will be sending the top of their order to the plate now, trying desperately to give Haddix a run to take into his final inning. After Ducky Schofield skies out to lead off, Bill Virdon breaks through for a single to center. Smoky Burgess flies out, but then Rocky Nelson comes through with a single to right which moves Virdon to third. Can Bob Skinner advance Virdon the final ninety feet? He meets a Burdette slider squarely and pulls it hard down the first-base line, but unfortunately right at Joe Adcock, who trots to the bag for the unassisted putout.

Haddix now cannot win this game in regulation time, but by retiring three more batters he can join the select ranks of those who have thrown a no-hitter and the far more exclusive club of perfect-game pitchers, of whom there have been only seven since major-league baseball began in 1876: John Richmond and Monte Ward in 1880, Cy Young in 1904, Addie Joss in 1908, Ernie Shore in 1917, Charley Robertson in 1922, and Don Larsen in 1956 (in the years to come, Jim Bunning, Sandy Koufax, and Catfish Hunter will also join the club).

Three outs to go. Haddix has been in this situation once before, on August 5, 1953, when as a St. Louis Cardinal he carried a no-hitter into the ninth against the Phils; Richie Ashburn led off with a single to right and wiped out that no-hit bid. And while still in the minors, with Columbus in the American Association, Haddix had once retired twenty-eight consecutive batters after allowing a hit in the first. But neither of those experiences could have prepared him for what is to come.

The home team is at bat. The fans want a win, of course, but they also want to be able to say that they witnessed a perfect game. This push and pull makes for an eerily quiet crowd as Haddix readies to pitch the bottom of the ninth. Up until now he has been pitching just as he would any other night (though with vastly superior results), but now he's determined to put everything he's got into getting his no-hitter. He still has no awareness of nearing a perfect game—he believes he walked a batter somewhere along the way. Giving his fastball a little extra, he fans Pafko to start the ninth. When Logan flies to Skinner, manager Fred Haney is put in a tough spot: Does he hit for Burdette and try to win the game in this inning, or virtually concede Haddix a perfect game by letting Lew bat, in the hope that the Braves can win in overtime?

Although surely not a soul in the stadium recalls it, manager Bill Murray of the Phils, back on July 4, 1908, was in precisely the same position. George "Hooks" Wiltse of the Giants had retired the first twenty-six Phils, but Phillies' pitcher George McQuillan was himself throwing a shutout. Murray allowed McQuillan to bat. After Wiltse threw the first two pitches for strikes, he followed with an 0–2 curveball that sailed and hit McQuillan in the back, destroying the perfect game (Wiltse kept his no-hitter, however, winning 1–0 in the tenth). Fred Haney was ten years old when that game was played, and you can be certain he is not reflecting back to it now; but his decision is the same as Murray's was: let the pitcher bat.

Burdette strikes out, and Haddix has done it—but no happy mob of well-wishers rushes out to clap him on the back, to lift him onto their shoulders. Haddix has been perfect, but thus far it has not been enough; the game must go on. He walks in from the mound, and in the relative privacy of the dugout his teammates do crowd about him and offer their congratulations. But backslapping is not enough now; the only show of appreciation that Haddix has any use for is a run.

After Mazeroski is retired, Hoak singles. Murtaugh calls back Mejias and sends Dick Stuart to the plate in his stead. Stuart is a 6'4" slugger who came up to Pittsburgh last year; in 1956 he hit 66 homers for Lincoln in the Western League. Burdette tries a curve; Stuart extends his long arms, takes a big, sweeping cut, and sends the ball soaring on a high arc to center, going, going . . . but not gone—the wind once again keeps a Pirate drive in the playing area, and Pafko camps under it for the out. Haddix, too, is retired, and now interest focuses on how much longer he can continue his perfect game.

For a man beset by a cold, Haddix has shown remarkable vigor, striking out eight in the first nine innings. But in the tenth he shows signs of wearing down, perhaps from the emotional as much as the physical strain. Del Rice—who had been Haddix's catcher in that near-no-hitter in 1953—bats for O'Brien and sends Virdon to the warning track to haul down his long drive. Mathews follows with a clout to virtually the same spot—some ten feet from the wire fence which encloses the outfield—and Virdon grabs that one, too. Aaron grounds to Schofield, and the burden of preserving the tie falls back on Burdette.

Schofield singles off Burdette's hand, and now it's up to Virdon to move him along with a sacrifice. But Bill bunts the ball out in front of the plate, where Crandall pounces on it and fires to second for the force. You can hear the groans—have the fans' sympathies shifted; do they now wish Haddix to win? Burgess raps a hard grounder to Adcock at the bag. He steps on first for one out and throws to Logan, who slaps the tag on the sliding Virdon.

Haddix just keeps rolling along—now that he's got the hang of it, it seems, he'll never give up another hit. In the eleventh he

Harvey Haddix fires a pitch to Eddie Mathews on his way to baseball immortality.

gets Adcock on a grounder and Covington and Crandall on flies to medium center. Besides being the first man ever to pitch a perfect game beyond nine innings, Haddix has now pitched the longest no-hit game on record, surpassing the ten and two-thirds hitless innings hurled by Harry McIntire in a losing effort in 1906.

Records, records—all Harvey wants out of this is a win. Yet in spite of a two-out single in the twelfth by Mazeroski, the Bucs once again fail to score. Harvey tightens his belt for one more go-round, and has a rather easy time with the bottom of the order: a tap to the box by Pafko, a fly to center by Logan, and a bouncer to third by Burdette, who is, let's not forget, pitching a whale of a game himself. Although he's allowed eleven hits (all singles), the key to his success tonight—as it is to Haddix's —is control: He has not walked a man. Lew tantalizes the Bucs by allowing another two-out single—this time to Schofield—before slamming the door shut again.

The tension of this game has been unrelieved for at least six innings now, to the point that it has begun to numb. Haddix and Burdette have been mowing down the batters as sharpshooters plug clay pigeons; something's *got* to give.

Murtaugh suggests to Haddix that he not go out for the thirteenth, that he be content with having pitched the greatest game of all time and let someone else worry about the win or the loss. But Harvey refuses. The first batter he will face in the thirteenth is Felix Mantilla, a twenty-four-year-old jack-of-all-positions and master of none who replaced O'Brien in the eleventh. Haddix gets two strikes on the slender second baseman, then zips one by him for what he thinks is a third strike—but umpire Vinnie Smith disagrees. On the next pitch Mantilla taps a bouncer to third. Hoak, Haddix's roommate, fields the ball easily, examines the seams of the ball and positions them to his liking, then throws the ball away. Nelson extends as far as he can on the infield side of first, but the ball bounces in the dirt, kicking off his foot. Rocky hurriedly picks up the ball and tags Mantilla, claiming he had rounded first with notions of going to second. But umpire Frank Dascoli is having none of that; and there stands Mantilla on first, after thirty-six batters in a row had failed to get there. The perfect game is no more, but the no-hitter lives.

Even with slugger Eddie Mathews at the plate, manager Haney calls for the bunt—and Eddie, though he is hardly ever called upon to lay one down, does so on the very first pitch he sees. Mantilla stands at second; first base is open; Henry Aaron, hitting .442 at this precise moment, is at the plate, and his run means nothing. The strategy is obvious: walk him and set up a possible double play on the lumbering Adcock. Until this intentional pass to Aaron, Haddix has gone behind on the count to only one batter—Andy Pafko, who in the twelfth took Harvey's first two pitches for balls.

Adcock watches the first pitch go by for ball one. The next pitch, Haddix's 115th of the game, is a slider ticketed for the low outside corner. But Haddix hangs the breaking ball up— "my only bad pitch," he will later declare, "the only mistake I made"—and Adcock blasts it to deep right center. As the fans rise to their feet with a shout, Virdon races to the fence and leaps; but the ball is gone, barely but fatally gone. The no-hitter, the shutout, the win, all are gone with it.

Haddix turns his view from the outfield back toward home and trudges sadly to the dugout. As he descends the steps, Adcock makes his way around the bases, knowing from first-base umpire Dascoli's wave of the hand that he has hit a home run. But Aaron, looking only at the flight of the ball, believes it landed in the warning track; after touching second base and seeing that Mantilla was across the plate, Henry cuts back across the infield toward the dugout. The jubilant Braves are all set to whoop it up in the locker room when Haney realizes that while the Pirates and Braves have left the field, the umpires are still standing out there.

In a flash he and his coaches grasp the situation and haul Aaron and Adcock back out onto the field to retrace their flawed steps toward home. Dascoli rules Adcock out for passing Aaron on the basepaths, but permits Aaron to score, making the final score 2–0. Tomorrow morning, National League president Warren Giles will pronounce the final score as 1–0, with Aaron not being permitted to advance beyond third base on Adcock's "double."

This helter-skelter resolution detracts from the elegance of the game, but the essence remains: On this May night in Milwaukee, perfection was not good enough. Harvey Haddix pitched the greatest game any pitcher has ever pitched, and in the end it was nothing but a loss, a gut-wrenching, heartbreaking loss.

May 26, 1959

PITTSBURGH	AB	R	H	P	A	E
Schofield, ss.	6	0	3	2	4	0
Virdon, cf.	6	0	1	8	0	0
Burgess, c.	5	0	0	8	0	0
Nelson, 1b.	5	0	2	14	0	0
Skinner, lf.	5	0	1	4	0	0
Mazeroski, 2b.	5	0	1	1	1	0
Hoak, 3b.	5	0	2	0	6	1
Mejias, rf.	3	0	1	1	0	0
a Stuart	1	0	0	0	0	0
Christopher, rf. ...	1	0	0	0	0	0
Haddix, p.	5	0	1	0	2	0
TOTALS	47	0	12	38	13	1

MILWAUKEE	AB	R	H	P	A	E
O'Brien, 2b.	3	0	0	2	5	0
b Rice	1	0	0	0	0	0
Mantilla, 2b.	1	1	0	1	2	0
Mathews, 3b.	4	0	0	2	3	0
Aaron, rf.	4	0	0	1	0	0
Adcock, 1b.	5	0	1	17	3	0
Covington, lf.	4	0	0	4	0	0
Crandall, c.	4	0	0	2	1	0
Pafko, cf.	4	0	0	6	0	0
Logan, ss.	4	0	0	3	5	0
Burdette, p.	4	0	0	1	3	0
TOTALS	38	1	1	39	22	0

a Flied out for Mejias in 10th
b Flied out for O'Brien in 10th

```
PITTSBURGH    000  000  000  000  0 — 0
MILWAUKEE     000  000  000  000  1 — 1
```

RBI—Adcock. 2B—Adcock. Sac.—Mathews. DP—Milw. 3. LOB—Pitt. 8, Milw. 1. Umpires—Smith, Dascoli, Secory, Dixon. Time—2:54. Att.—19,194.

PITTSBURGH	IP	H	R	ER	BB	SO
Haddix	12⅔	1	1	0	1	8

MILWAUKEE						
Burdette	13	12	0	0	0	2

Pittsburgh Pirates vs. Milwaukee Braves   *131*

October 13, 1960
New York Yankees
vs.
Pittsburgh Pirates

Witnessing a perfect game is a once-in-a-lifetime thrill; seeing two of them back to back may be too much of a good thing.
Even the baseball purist, for whom pitching is 80 percent of the
game, likes a base hit now and then. So, for a change of pace,
let's go to Forbes Field in Pittsburgh where the Pirates and the
Yankees, the teams for which Haddix and Larsen toiled so nobly,
are all set to embark upon the wildest seventh game in World
Series history.

Neither team made it to the fall classic last year. For New
York it was a shock; for Pittsburgh, a tradition. While this
year's Yankee pennant was Stengel's tenth in twelve years, the

Bucs had not won a flag since 1927, and in that World Series they had had the misfortune to face the Murderers' Row Yankees, who demolished them in four straight. This year's edition of the Bronx Bombers has demolished the Pirates in Games Two, Three, and Six by the preposterous scores of 16–3, 10–0, and 12–0.

However, the Pirates have somehow managed to win three games of their own, by conventional margins, and need not be embarrassed to show up today. Although the Yankees have certainly been more impressive, these two teams are closer in ability than the scores of the Yankee victories would lead you to suspect. If we examine the teams position by position you'll see what I mean. (Some of the players will be familiar from the previous two games we've attended, but there are quite a few new faces.)

First base: The Pirates this year have fielded a combination of their rising young slugging star Dick Stuart and the veteran Rocky Nelson. Both had fine 1960 seasons, combining for 30 home runs and 118 RBI's, but Stuart has been a bust in the Series thus far. The Yankee first sacker is Bill "Moose" Skowron, in his seventh year with the team, yet only his first as a full-timer. He pounded out 26 homers and drove in 91. Though the Pirate combination was more productive, we must weigh Skowron against Nelson, who will get the start today. Both hit over .300; Nelson is the superior fielder; but the overall edge goes to *Skowron.*

Second base: After a wretched 1959 season in which he hit .241 and moved sluggishly in the field because of overweight, Bill Mazeroski bounced back to hit a solid .273 and lead National League second basemen in glovework. Bobby Richardson of the Yankees, though no slouch in the field, is not the equal of Maz; at the plate he hit for a lower average and showed none of the Pirate's power. In the Series, however, Richardson has been a colossus, batting .360 with an unbelievable, record-setting 12 RBI's through the first six games. Nonetheless, edge: *Mazeroski*.

Shortstop: Dick Groat had a splendid season, batting .325 to top the lists; he will later be named Most Valuable Player in the National League. The prematurely bald twenty-nine-year-old is the team's leader and its only link among the regulars to the legendary 1952 Pirates who lost 112 games. A Lew Burdette pitch broke his wrist in September, and he just got off the shelf for the Series. The New York shortstop, Tony Kubek, is an average hitter and an average gloveman who, like his double-play partner, is hitting out of his mind in this Series—.370. Still, the edge belongs to *Groat*.

Third base: Though he led National League hot-corner men in errors, Don Hoak had a fine season at the plate while playing in all of his team's games. He will finish second to Groat in the MVP balloting. New York's third baseman sometimes is veteran Gil McDougald, slowing down in what will be his final year, and other times, twenty-two-year-old Clete Boyer, who makes phenomenal plays in the field but hit only .242. Boyer will start today. The edge goes to *Hoak*.

Left field: Bob Skinner had an okay year, .273 with 15 homers and 86 ribbies, but the Pirates had hoped for better. Struck by a Ryne Duren fastball in Game One, he will play today for the first time since then; his replacement in Games Two through Six has been Gino Cimoli. The Yankee left fielder this season has most often been Hector Lopez; but after Elston Howard hit a two-run pinch homer in the Series opener, Casey Stengel decided that a place had to be found for Howard's bat. So Howard moved behind the plate, where he had played most of the season, and Yogi Berra moved out to left field—that is, until the Pirates started a left-hander in Game Three, which put Berra on the bench and put Bob Cerv in left. Madness? That's

Stengel's method; at one point in the Series he even had Kubek playing left. Today Yogi is out there; and though he's thirty-five and starting to fade, he is still a dangerous hitter. In 200 fewer at bats than Skinner, he hit the same number of homers and knocked in only 24 fewer runs. Edge: *Berra.*

Center field: Virdon for the Bucs, Mantle for the Yanks. Though Virdon is superior in the field, this one is no contest: edge, *Mantle.*

Right field: Injured at the time of the perfect game in Milwaukee last year, Roberto Clemente has been healthy this season and will be out there today. An excellent fielder with a cannon for an arm, he is twenty-six years old and is just beginning to come into his prime. In 1960 he hit .314 with 16 homers and 94 RBI's. In the next twelve years he will hit under .300 only once, hit over .350 three times, and reach the 3,000-hit plateau. Like Mantle and Berra, Clemente is a Hall-of-Famer. New York's match for him is Roger Maris, acquired this year from Kansas City. Also a first-rate outfielder, though perhaps a notch below Clemente, Maris had a magnificent Yankee debut, belting 39 homers and leading the league with 112 RBI's; he will be named American League MVP this winter. Next year he will smash 61 homers to break Babe Ruth's record and will up his RBI total to 142. This is the hardest position to evaluate: Clemente will prove the superior player over the long haul, but Maris may be the more valuable right now. I have to call this one *even.*

Catcher: Pittsburgh, too, made a valuable acquisition from Kansas City this year—Hal Smith, who divides the catching with Smoky Burgess. Both are fine hitters—the right-handed Smith at .295, the left-handed Burgess one point lower—but unexceptional receivers. The Yanks have featured a three-man platoon during the season of Yogi Berra, John Blanchard, and, most often, Elston Howard. But Howard was hit by a pitch in the

Roberto Clemente was a natural, a once-in-a-generation player who not only did everything brilliantly, but did it with style. In this World Series he has begun to attract the national attention he craves and deserves.

second inning of yesterday's game, and Blanchard came in to go 3-for-4 with a pair of doubles; he gets the starting nod today. Edge: *Burgess.*

Pitcher: New York had the top pitching staff in the American League while Pittsburgh's was only third best in the National; yet the Pirate starters are at least the equal of the New Yorkers, and they have in Roy Face a bullpen ace the Yanks cannot match. Today's game will pit two thirty-year-old right-handers. Pittsburgh will go with its 20-game winner, Vern "Deacon" Law, who, despite hurting his ankle five days before the Series opener, has managed to win two games, each with help from Face. His opponent will be Bullet Bob Turley, who came to the Yanks in the 1954 deal that also involved, oddly enough, both Don Larsen and Pirate catcher Hal Smith, then Yankee property. In 1958 Turley was a 21-game winner and the hero of the World Series. In the last two seasons, however, his fastball has lost its steam and he has struggled with his control, winning only 17 in 1959 and 1960 combined. Though he pitched well to win Game Two, the edge here is decidedly with *Law.*

Were you wondering what happened to Haddix and Larsen? After his perfect game, Harvey went right back to being a .500 pitcher. He started and won Game Five of the Series, and will be in the bullpen today if needed. Larsen, sadly, is not here this afternoon. In the next three seasons after his masterpiece, he won only 25 games for the Yankees and was packed off to Kansas City in the deal which brought Roger Maris to New York. By the first week in July of 1960 his record with the last-place A's was 1–10, and he was sent down to the American Association.

Now that we have evaluated the two squads, what do we come up with? Four positions at which the Pirates have an edge, four at which the advantage lies with New York, and one that is even. The scores of the Yankees' three victories would lead you to think that the Pirates don't belong on the same field with them; but now we see that if ever a Series deserved to go the full seven games, it is this one. Even the home-field advantage, which now should swing to Pittsburgh, has been nullified in this Series: the Pirates have won two of the three games played in Yankee Stadium, and New York has taken two of three here.

Forbes Field has been home to the Pirates since 1909, and of the sixteen major-league parks it is second in age only to Philadelphia's Shibe Park. Its seating capacity is small—33,730—but its dimensions are mammoth: 365 down the line in left, 435 to dead center, and 457 at a point just left of center. Down the line in right, the wall is only 300 feet from home, but a 27-foot-high screen deters cheap homers. In the power alleys, a batter whose heart is set on a home run must drive the ball 406 feet in left center and 416 feet in right center. Old Forbes is a fine place to watch a game, as we shall see from our bleacher seats on the line in left, alongside the 12-foot-high ivy-covered wall.

Bobby Richardson will be the leadoff batter in the opening frame. Little Bobby, 5'9" and 170 pounds, belted a grand-slam homer in Game Three and added two more RBI's later in that contest to set a record. Once again he meets the ball squarely and lines it hard, but right at Groat. Kubek pops one to Mazeroski. Maris lifts one to Hoak, and Law has passed his first test.

Turley starts out in similar fashion, getting Virdon to fly to left and Groat to pop up to short. But then Bullet Bob walks Skinner and grooves a pitch to cleanup batter Rocky Nelson, who deposits it neatly over the screen in right. The Bucs are up by 2–0, and the fans are delighted—Law allowed only two runs in each of his previous starts in the Series and looked strong in his first inning today.

He is equally strong in the second, putting the side down in order with the aid of a fine stop by Hoak of Berra's grounder. But Turley's troubles continue: Burgess rips the ball down the first-base line. Only the combination of Maris's fast fielding and

Rocky Nelson is a nomad. In addition to seven minor-league stops, he has played for: the Cardinals, Pirates, White Sox, Dodgers, Indians, Dodgers again, Cards again, and finally, the Pirates . . . again.

Burgess's slow legs holds the hit to a single. Stengel has seen enough of Turley for today. Ordinarily Old Case is not so quick with the hook; but he sees that his boys are having a tough time with Law, and being two runs down already is bad enough. Out of the bullpen comes Bill Stafford, a twenty-one-year-old right-hander recalled from Richmond in August. Three days ago he pitched five innings of scoreless relief, but today he gets out of the starting blocks poorly. He walks Hoak on four pitches, then is too late with his throw to first on Mazeroski's bunt, loading the bases. Now the Yankees get a break—Law raps one right back to Stafford, who throws home to Blanchard for one out, who in turn fires to first for the twin killing. That should break the back of the rally, but it doesn't: Virdon singles to right center, scoring Hoak and Mazeroski, and when Maris fumbles the ball, Bill takes another base. Forbes Field is really rocking now—long-suffering Pirate fans can smell their first championship in thirty-five years. Groat grounds to Boyer to end the inning—but who needs more than four runs with Law on the mound? The Deacon makes easy work of the Yanks in the third despite allowing his first hit, a two-out single to Hector Lopez, batting for Stafford.

The new man on the hill for New York is little Bobby Shantz, a 5'6", 140-pound left-hander who once won 24 games and the MVP Award while in the employ of the Philadelphia A's. Bobby is thirty-five now and no longer a star, but this past year he was the Yankees' top reliever, posting 11 saves and 5 wins. Ordinarily you wouldn't expect to see him until the late innings, but Casey feels he has to go with his best right now; Pittsburgh must not tally again. And Shantz obliges, getting Skinner on a grounder and, after walking Nelson, inducing Clemente to hit into a double play.

Law stays on the beam in the next inning, but the Yankees do begin to hint at a little offense. After Kubek pops to short,

Maris lines hard to right. Mantle follows with a single to right and Berra with a fly to right. Clemente has had to handle three straight chances, all pulled, all well hit.

Shantz disposes of the Pirates on three infield outs in the fourth, and the Yankees finally take Law into their own hands. Skowron, too, hits the ball to right, the difference being that this one does not come down in Clemente's glove; instead, it drops into the lower right-field seats. The gap is narrowed, but solo home runs are not going to get the Yankees back in the ballgame—they need base runners. And base runners are not yet to be had, as Blanchard flies to center, Boyer lines to Maz, and Shantz pops to Nelson.

Pirate manager Danny Murtaugh realized before the game that Law's tender ankle would probably start to give him trouble in the middle innings, as it did in Games One and Four. Still, he'd like the Deacon to give him six or seven innings so that short-relief ace Roy Face can finish up. Face has already saved each of Pittsburgh's three victories in the Series, recording sixteen outs without allowing a hit in the last two wins.

After Shantz puts the Pirates down harmlessly in the fifth, Richardson opens the New York sixth with a single to center. When the next batter, Kubek, walks, Murtaugh decides to act. Law heads to the dugout as the fans give him a hand, and in comes Face. A right-hander not much bigger than Shantz, Roy is only 5'8" and 155 pounds. He is coming off a year in which he recorded 24 saves and 10 wins and was every bit as effective as he had been in 1959, that incredible year when he went 18–1 and stretched his two-season winning streak to 22 games. Though he does throw a fastball and curve, the pitch on which Face bases his fame is the forkball, delivered by wrapping the index and middle fingers around the ball where there are no seams. It slips out of Face's hand with little or no rotation, and, like its disreputable cousin, the spitter, it drops explosively at the last instant, yielding a ground ball.

Roy does get his ground ball—but not when he wants it. First, Maris goes out on a foul pop to Hoak. Then Mantle wallops a skidding scorcher up the middle that Groat cannot stop; Richardson scores and Kubek goes to third. The next batter is Berra, a notorious bad-ball hitter whose uppercut swing has scooped pitches off the ground and into the seats. Face sends him a forkball, and Yogi reaches down and whacks it, high along the right-field line. Fair by inches, the blast lands in the upper deck—and the Yankees go out in front, 5–4. The Pirate lead has evaporated, and now the game is in danger of blowing wide

Roy Face

open. Here Murtaugh shows faith in his fireman, leaving him in to get Skowron on a foul to Hoak, and Blanchard on the long-sought ground ball.

The fans are in a state of shock as the teams exchange places. And when Shantz sets the Bucs down in order yet again, the quiet in Forbes Field is deafening. While the Pirates' celebrated relief star has been bombed, Shantz has now gone four innings without allowing a hit and has faced the minimum twelve batters.

As if Shantz had not done enough already, Stengel lets him bat in the seventh with one man out and he bounces a single into left. But Face bears down now, retiring Richardson and Kubek and keeping the Pirate deficit at one run.

If you were surprised that Murtaugh left Face in to pitch the top of the seventh, you will find it equally hard to swallow that he permits left-handed Burgess to lead off against Shantz in the bottom of the seventh. Nevertheless, just as Face pitched a scoreless seventh, now Burgess singles to center—Murtaugh may be playing hunches, or he may be catnapping on the bench, but he gets results and that's all that counts. Joe Christopher comes in to run for Burgess and, after Hoak lines out to Berra, is doubled up on Mazeroski's groundout.

Face reappears for the eighth, along with new battery-mate Hal Smith. Maris, having a rough day, dribbles one back to the mound; and when Mantle follows with a liner to Groat, all seems serene. But now Face, understandably reluctant to groove one to Berra, walks him. Skowron sends a high hopper to third and beats it out, Yogi advancing one base. Now comes the crucial out, and Face can't get it: Blanchard lines a hard single to right center, bringing home Berra and pushing Skowron to third. *Still* Face stays in—is it simply because he's due to lead off the bottom of the eighth, and Murtaugh doesn't want to waste an arm for one-third of an inning's work? Boyer doubles to the left-field corner, with Skowron scoring and Blanchard going to third. The Yanks will take at least a three-run lead into the bottom of the eighth, perhaps more if Stengel puts up a hitter for Shantz, now scheduled to bat. Bobby's pitched five full frames already, surely as long as he's gone all year. But he's shown no sign of tiring, so Casey lets him bat; he ends the inning with a fly to right.

Gino Cimoli, a reserve outfielder who hit .267 this year, bats for Face and loops a single into right center. A rally? No, for Virdon raps a perfect double-play ball to Kubek. Tony comes in a step, bends, and—the ball kicks up over his glove right into his Adam's apple! He goes down as if he were shot, clutching his throat, while the ball rolls away. Richardson retrieves the ball, but not in time to make a play. The Yankee trainer rushes out to attend to Kubek, who is in terrible pain and must come out of the ball game. He is replaced at short by Joe DeMaestri, another player who came to New York from K.C. in the Larsen-Maris trade.

The Pirates do have a rally stirring after all: Instead of two outs with no one on base, they find themselves with two men on and no one out. Lady Luck has smiled on the Pirates; now it's up to them to make something of their break. And Groat does, driving a single through the hole into left which scores Cimoli and sends Virdon to second. The tying runs are now on base, and Forbes Field, a tomb a moment ago, is rocking once more. Out strolls Stengel to take the ball from Shantz and hand it on to Jim Coates. A lanky 6′4″ right-hander who divided his time between starting chores and the bullpen in 1960, Coates was hit rather freely yet posted a fine mark of 13–3. With left-handed Bob Skinner the first man Coates will face, Stengel's move flies in the face of the percentages, in which he became an expert as a disciple of John McGraw in the early 1920s.

Skinner bunts both runners up into scoring position, and now it's up to Nelson, the minor-league batting king who has at last discovered his major-league batting eye. Coates burns in a fastball, and Rocky gets under it, lifting a fly to shallow right; both runners hold. Two outs, and the pressure shifts to Clemente, who's had a fine first six games but has been throttled today. Hitting a breaking pitch off the end of his bat, Roberto tops a slow bouncer to first, where Skowron is playing deep; Moose gloves the ball, looks up to make the throw to the pitcher covering . . . but Coates has not left the mound! Virdon scores to bring the Bucs back within one run, and Groat takes third.

The batter now is Hal Smith, 2-for-7 in the Series with no RBI's. Coates battles him to a count of 2–2, then fires a fastball in belt-high. Smith swings with everything he's got and lashes

Hal Smith

the ball to deep left center. Berra races a few steps along the length of the ivy-draped wall to the 406-foot marker, then halts his pursuit. The ball flies over the wall, sending all Pittsburgh into pandemonium. Smith crosses the plate with the Bucs' fifth run of the inning, and the team that looked to be out of the running at 7–4 now leads 9–7 with only three outs to go!

But there's still one more Pirate to be retired in the eighth: exit Coates, enter Ralph Terry. This twenty-four-year-old right-hander has, despite his tender years, been around. He broke in with New York in 1956, was dealt to Kansas City the following year, then was reacquired by the Yankees on May 26, 1959—the date of Haddix's perfect game. This has been his first winning year: 10–8, mostly as a starter. Terry retires Don Hoak on a fly to left, and we go into the ninth with the Yankees needing two to tie.

Whom will Murtaugh select to protect the lead now that Face is out of the game? Passing over his accustomed relievers, Danny brings on Bob Friend, the Bucs' top winner behind Law, and a man who has been with the franchise since the bad old days of 1951–52. But Bob relieved only once during the season, and was the losing pitcher yesterday (12–0) and in Game Two (16–3).

The first man Friend must face is Richardson, who already has eleven hits in this Series and is one shy of the record held by his second-base predecessor, Billy Martin. Bobby finds a serve to his liking and strokes it out into left center, tying the record and, more important, bringing the tying run to the plate. De Maestri is due up, but Stengel replaces him with Dale Long, a thirty-four-year-old reserve first baseman who is notable in baseball history for two accomplishments: (1) while a member of the Pirates in 1956, he clouted a home run a day for eight straight days; and (2) in 1958 while with the Cubs he became, for two games, the only left-handed catcher in this century. Baseball trivia aside, Long does present a threat. Though he fails to crank out the long ball this time, Dale does manage a single to right which pushes Richardson up one base and pushes Friend out of the ball game.

With Maris, Mantle, and Berra due up, a left-hander would seem called for, not only to counter Maris and Berra, but also to make switch-hitter Mantle bat from the right side and take aim at the more distant wall in left. Murtaugh has Joe Gibbon, he has Vinegar Bend Mizell, he has Fred Green, and he has— Harvey Haddix, who is on his way in right now. Can he make up today for the crushing disappointment of that night in Milwaukee last year?

He gets off to a good start, as Maris fouls out to Smith behind the plate. But Mantle rips a single to right center, scoring Richardson and sending Long, not a fast man, to third. (Casey has been sleeping, I think: Only now that Long has reached third does he send McDougald in to run for him.) The batter is Berra. Haddix feeds him a breaking ball, and Yogi blasts a two-hop grounder down the first-base line. Nelson makes a great backhanded stop behind first base; but the ball is hit so hard that it spins him around, and when he turns back to the infield he is confused. McDougald is coming in with the tying run, but it won't count if Rocky can set in motion a first-to-second-to-first double play. Rocky, however, looks to home plate, decides he can't make a play there, then races to first and steps on the bag, retiring Berra. This takes the force off Mantle at second. Mickey, though, never got farther than a few steps from first, fearing that Yogi's shot would be caught in the air. So, as Nelson steps on first, pivots, and looks up the base path to make the throw to second base—Mantle is diving back into first. Nelson swipes a tag at Mantle, but it is too late. He is safe, and the tying run is in. Skowron follows this farcical ballet with a grounder to Groat, who flips to Mazeroski for the force.

It is the bottom of the ninth. McDougald comes in to play third base, Boyer moves over to short, and Ralph Terry returns to the mound. The scheduled batters are Mazeroski, Haddix, and Virdon. The key for Terry in this frame will be to keep Mazeroski off base and thus (a) deny Haddix the opportunity to advance him with a bunt and (b) force Murtaugh to decide whether or not to hit for Haddix.

As Mazeroski walks to the plate, all he thinks to himself is, "Get on base"; in the seventh inning he had gone for the long ball, overswung, and hit into a double play. Yet deep in his mind, he is to confess in later years, "I thought we were going to lose. You couldn't feel too bad to take the Yankees to the seventh game and lose in extra innings." Maz is guessing fastball, and is prepared to let other pitches go by until he has two strikes on him. The first pitch is indeed a fastball, but it is too high. Ball one. Terry's next offering is the pitcher's nightmare—the slider that doesn't slide, hanging up high looking for all the world like a Little Leaguer's fastball. The ball crosses the plate at the letters, Mazeroski swings, and the rest is history. With Berra once again giving futile chase, the ball sails over the left-field wall and ignites Forbes Field into bedlam. As Maz circles the bases in joyful astonishment, fans come streaming down onto

There is delirium on the basepaths as Bill Mazeroski is about to give Pittsburgh its first world's championship in thirty-five years. Though he will play twelve more seasons, nothing will come close to the thrill of this homer.

the field, into the base path between third and home. What is Maz thinking as he nears the plate? "I was too excited and thrilled to think," he will say after the game. "It was the greatest moment in my life."

Not so for the Yankees, who outscored the Bucs 55–27, outhit them 91–60, outhomered them 10–4, and batted an incredible .338 to Pittsburgh's .254—all for naught. And certainly not for Ralph Terry, the goat, who instantly took his place alongside Ralph Branca in the Hall of Blame. But unlike Branca, Terry will get a chance to redeem himself in a big game. Given the start in Game Seven of the 1962 World Series, he will win it with a shutout.

October 13, 1960

NEW YORK

	AB	R	H	P	A	E
Richardson, 2b. ...	5	2	2	2	5	0
Kubek, ss.	3	1	0	3	2	0
DeMaestri, ss.	0	0	0	0	0	0
d Long	1	0	1	0	0	0
e McDougald, 3b. ..	0	1	0	0	0	0
Maris, rf.	5	0	0	2	0	1
Mantle, cf.	5	1	3	0	0	0
Berra, lf.	4	2	1	3	0	0
Skowron, 1b.	5	2	2	10	2	0
Blanchard, c.	4	0	1	1	1	0
Boyer, 3b.-ss.	4	0	1	0	3	0
Turley, p.	0	0	0	0	0	0
Stafford, p.	0	0	0	0	1	0
a Lopez	1	0	1	0	0	0
Shantz, p.	3	0	1	3	1	0
Coates, p.	0	0	0	0	0	0
Terry, p.	0	0	0	0	0	0
TOTALS	40	9	13	24	15	1

PITTSBURGH

	AB	R	H	P	A	E
Virdon, cf.	4	1	2	3	0	0
Groat, ss.	4	1	1	3	2	0
Skinner, lf.	2	1	0	1	0	0
Nelson, 1b.	3	1	1	7	0	0
Clemente, rf.	4	1	1	4	0	0
Burgess, c.	3	0	2	0	0	0
b Christopher	0	0	0	0	0	0
Smith, c.	1	1	1	1	0	0
Hoak, 3b.	3	1	0	3	2	0
Mazeroski, 2b.	4	2	2	5	0	0
Law, p.	2	0	0	0	1	0
Face, p.	0	0	0	0	1	0
c Cimoli	1	1	1	0	0	0
Friend, p.	0	0	0	0	0	0
Haddix, p.	0	0	0	0	0	0
TOTALS	31	10	11	27	6	0

a Singled for Stafford in 3rd
b Ran for Burgess in 7th
c Singled for Face in 8th
d Singled for DeMaestri in 9th
e Ran for Long in 9th

NEW YORK	000	014	022 — 9
PITTSBURGH	220	000	051 — 10

RBI—Mantle 2, Berra 4, Skowron, Blanchard, Boyer, Virdon 2, Nelson 2, Smith 3, Groat, Clemente, Mazeroski. 2B—Boyer. HR—Nelson, Skowron, Berra, Smith, Mazeroski. Sac.—Skinner. DP—N.Y. 3. LOB—N.Y. 6, Pitt. 1. Umpires—Jackowski, Chylak, Boggess, Stevens, Landes, Honochick. Time—2:36. Att.—36,683.

NEW YORK	IP	H	R	ER	BB	SO
*Turley	1	2	3	3	1	0
Stafford	1	2	1	1	1	0
***Shantz	5	4	3	3	1	0
Coates	⅔	2	2	2	0	0
*****Terry (L)	⅓	1	1	1	0	0
PITTSBURGH						
**Law	5	4	3	3	1	0
Face	3	6	4	4	1	0
****Friend	0	2	2	2	0	0
Haddix (W)	1	1	0	0	0	0

*Pitched to one batter in 2nd
**Pitched to two batters in 6th
***Pitched to three batters in 8th
****Pitched to two batters in 9th
*****Pitched to one batter in 9th

October 21, 1975
Cincinnati Reds
vs.
Boston Red Sox

After three days of drenching rains the storm clouds have lifted at last, and there will be baseball in Boston tonight: Game Six of the 1975 World Series, a game and a Series which many will call the greatest ever played. Let's head out to historic Fenway Park and see whether we agree.

Built on an odd-sized lot in the Back Bay section of Boston, Fenway is a small park (capacity 33,379), an old one (1912), and an ugly one (from the outside resembling a nineteenth-century New England textile factory)—but it is a wonderful place to watch a ball game. With Detroit's Tiger Stadium and Chicago's venerable pair of Wrigley Field and Comiskey Park,

Fenway is a survivor from the days when stadiums were designed to put spectators right on top of the action. Modern arenas are more convenient to get into and out of, provide more comfortable accommodations, and have flashier scoreboards; but they don't have the *feel* of the old parks, the sense that you can reach out and touch the players, that the players, for being close, are real people like you and me.

Columbia Park, Griffith Stadium, Shibe Park, the Polo Grounds, the original Yankee Stadium, Forbes Field—six of the eight ball parks we've visited together—are gone, along with Ebbets Field, Sportsman's Park, Crosley Field, and many others. All have been replaced by gleaming new bowls which boast uniform dimensions and, all too often, artificial turf. But Fenway remains, not as a crumbling relic, but as a treasure house of tradition linking generations of Red Sox, from Tris Speaker and Babe Ruth to Carl Yastrzemski and Fred Lynn.

With its eccentric, seventeen-sided playing area and unusual dimensions—the outfield is deeper in right center than it is in dead center, for example—Fenway Park has been virtually a tenth player in the Boston lineup. Before this Series began, the Cincinnati players seemed far more concerned about how they might defeat Boston's "Green Monster"—the thirty-seven-foot-high wall in left that makes pop flies into homers and line-drive homers into singles—than they were about defeating Boston's Red Sox.

That was understandable, of course, because no one thought that the Sox belonged in the same park with the Reds. The Big Red Machine, as the men from Cincinnati were called, had rolled over its opposition in the National League, winning the divisional title by a staggering twenty games—the widest margin since 1906—and sweeping the Championship Series from Pittsburgh. A tremendous all-around club, the Reds led the National League in runs, in stolen bases, and in fielding percentage. Of the eight regulars in their lineup, three have already won Most Valuable Player honors and a fourth will go on to do so; five will probably make it to the Hall of Fame.

The Reds' weak link—and it is weak only in comparison with their strengths—is their starting pitchers, none of whom won more than fifteen games. (Don't they remind you of the 1924 Giants?) Yet even this shortcoming is counterbalanced by another strength: the busiest and best bullpen in baseball, which in fact forms the heart of the Cincinnati mound staff. So effective was this four-man relief squad that Red starters completed a mere twenty-two games, an all-time low for a pennant-winning team. So ready is manager Sparky Anderson to yank his starter (and any reliever who falters for so much as an instant) that he has been given the nickname "Captain Hook."

The "experts" figured that Boston would take perhaps one and no more than two games from these midwestern maulers. But the Red Sox have already taken two, and the truth is that with a break they might have closed out the Series in four straight. In Game Two they led with two out in the ninth, and Game Four was settled in extra innings on a hotly disputed decision by an umpire. But the breaks did not come; both games were lost by a single run, and Boston must win tonight or the Series is over.

The Red Sox are underdogs because the Reds are awesome, not because they themselves are a poor team. They did, after all, end the three-year reign of the Oakland A's, no mean feat. Their team batting average of .275 was the best in the majors, better even than that of the Reds. And they, too, have good power, solid defense, and adequate starting pitchers. But unlike Cincinnati, the Red Sox cannot or will not run, and their bullpen is suspect.

Let's find seats in back of first base tonight; that spot will give us a good view of any balls hit toward The Monster over in left and of the man who plays left field in Fenway more brilliantly than anyone ever has, Carl Yastrzemski. Yaz, who broke in as a twenty-one-year-old in 1961, today forms a major link with the past: He is the man who replaced the great Ted Williams, and he is one of only two current Red Sox who played on their last championship team in 1967. In that year he won Triple Crown and MVP honors, and batted over .500 in the closing weeks of a white-hot pennant race.

Standing in center, tossing the ball with Yaz, is a rookie who looks to be the next great Boston star, Fred Lynn. All he did this year was to hit .331, belt 21 homers, drive home 105 runs, and collect a league-leading 47 doubles. His fellow freshman head-liner, Jim Rice, is sidelined for the Series with a broken hand, a terrible blow to Red Sox hopes.

Right-fielder Dwight Evans is also young, twenty-four, and in only his second season as a regular. Though he batted .274, his primary value to the team is his defense: Few can go get 'em as well as he can, and his arm can be compared with those of Carl Furillo and Roberto Clemente.

The Sox infield is not nearly as impressive, but still solid. At third is Rico Petrocelli, the shortstop on the '67 club, but now, at the age of thirty-two, in his final days as a big-leaguer. The current shortstop is a youngster, Rick "Rooster" Burleson, who covers a lot of ground but makes too many throwing errors, a problem he will correct with experience. At second is a veteran, Denny Doyle; his early-season acquisition from the Angels may have been the one move that lifted the Sox from also-rans to pennant winners. And at first is Cecil Cooper, a tall left-hander who hit .311 as the designated hitter through most of the season while Yastrzemski played first, but is in the field now because of the injury to Rice.

Behind the plate crouches 6'3" Carlton Fisk, New England born, New England bred, and New England's favorite son on the Red Sox. "Pudge" was idle through the first half of the season with a broken hand, then came back in the final seventy-nine games to hit a resounding .331, his best mark ever. He is warming up the old man, Luis Tiant, listed as thirty-four but rumored to have fought in the Spanish-American War. A fast-balling right-hander with Cleveland in the late 1960s, El Tiante hurt his arm and saw his career take a tailspin: In less than two months in the spring of 1971, he was given his unconditional release by the Twins, picked up by the pitching-poor Braves, and then released by *them*. Two years later he was a 20-game winner for Boston —no longer relying on the fastball, but now disguising it

Luis Tiant

amid a variety of breaking pitches, paces, and angles of delivery. His gyrations, revolutions, and pirouettes on the mound delight the spectators and baffle the hitters. He blanked the Reds in Game One and struggled through 163 pitches to win a tense Game Four.

The night is cool and clear, the full moon glistens over the right-field bleachers, and Pete Rose is standing in the batter's box. Pete has hit over .300 ten times in the last eleven seasons (a streak he will continue in the years to follow), and 1975 was a typically fine year. However, he is only 1-for-7 against Tiant thus far; in the opener, he took the toughest "ofer" (0-for-4) you ever saw, each of his four outs a blast right at somebody. Tonight his bad luck continues: Yastrzemski, playing a shallow left field, races in at the crack of the bat and dives, snatching Rose's humpbacked liner as he slides on the still-damp sod.

Next up is Ken Griffey, the superspeedster whose .305 average was built up by the amazing total of thirty-five infield hits. He walks. But will he run? The Reds have stolen bases on their last six attempts. None of these bases, though, was stolen while Tiant was on the mound; Looie has a great pickoff move which keeps the runners close. Griffey holds while the next two batters, Joe Morgan and Johnny Bench, are retired. Of the men Cincinnati has sent to the plate in the first, Rose has won one Most Valuable Player Award, Bench has won two, and Morgan will win this year and next!

Now let's look at the Reds in the field. Their outfield consists of Griffey in right, an average defensive player; George Foster in left, likewise; and Cesar Geronimo in center, an exceptional fielder with a shotgun arm. The Reds acquired Foster from the Giants in a deal that was truly a steal; hypnosis cured him of his fear of inside pitches, and now he is a rising star, also destined to become a National League MVP. Geronimo is a light hitter, the only one in the lineup, but his glove saves so many runs that all he has to hit is .250.

The infield is exceptional. First baseman Tony Perez, thirty-three years old and the inspirational leader of the club, drives in ninety or more runs year after year. In Game Four his two home runs led the Reds to victory. At second is Joe Morgan, the complete offensive weapon: this season, a .317 average, 17 homers, 94 RBI's, 107 runs, 132 walks, and 67 steals. If this were not enough, the 5'7" sparkplug is also the top-fielding second baseman in baseball. Shortstop Dave Concepcion is an exceptional gloveman, too, with phenomenal range, and at the bat he is improving steadily. Third base is occupied by Pete Rose, whose installation there on May 3 opened up a spot in left field for

Foster and really set the Big Red Machine in motion. Through hard work Pete has made himself competent at the hot corner.

The backstop is perennial All-Star Johnny Bench, only twenty-seven, yet in his ninth year with the Reds. He is coming off an "ordinary" year for him—28 homers, 110 RBI's. On the mound is Gary Nolan, a right-hander who came to the majors the same year as Bench. At eighteen he was a strikeout star with explosive speed; then he, like Tiant, hurt his arm, lost his fastball, and was written off as washed up— in 1973–74 combined, he was

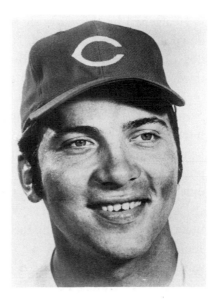

Johnny Bench

able to pitch only ten innings. In 1975, however, at age twenty-seven, he returned to stardom as a curveball-and-control pitcher, going 15–9.

Nolan gets off to a fast start, retiring Cooper on a fly to center and Doyle on a grounder to first. But then Yaz and Fisk single, and Freddie Lynn brings Boston fans to their feet as he drives a pitch deep into right-center field. He is slow to get out of the box, lagging to watch the flight of the ball. As it settles into the bleachers and the crowd erupts, he smacks his hands together in satisfaction and starts on his tour of the bases. Three runs already—there will be a tomorrow after all! The crowd hardly settles back in its seats before Rico Petrocelli hoists them back up with a blast to deep left center; but this one stays in the park, and anything in the park, Geronimo catches.

Heartened by this early show of support, Tiant sets the Reds down in order in the second. Nolan recovers his composure and does the same, fanning two. But when Gary is due to bat in the third, Captain Hook sends up a pinch hitter.

The Reds do not score in the third, and left-hander Fred Norman, 12–4 as a starter during the season, is the new Red pitcher. He debuts by getting Cooper on a pop to Concepcion behind third base, but then allows a double to Denny Doyle. Yaz pops out, and Anderson orders an intentional pass to Fisk, the only right-handed batter of the first five in the order. The strategy backfires, however, when Norman issues an unintentional pass to Lynn, loading the bases. Good-bye, Norman; hello, Jack Billingham, a righty who pitched well in Game Two and was upset when he was passed over for tonight's start. He closes the crisis by fanning Petrocelli.

El Tiante continues to throttle the Big Red Machine through the fourth, but Billingham courts disaster: Evans whacks a ground-rule double to right and Burleson draws a walk on four pitches, both with none out. Despite Tiant's successful bunt, advancing both runners, Jack pitches out of the jam, getting Cooper and Doyle on grounders while Evans dies on third.

In the fifth it is the Reds' turn to show some life. After Geronimo flies to right, Ed Armbrister bats for Billingham and draws a walk. Rose, now thoroughly familiar with Tiant's bag of tricks, lines a single to center that pushes Armbrister around to third. Now Griffey steps in for his licks. The Boston infield plays back, willing to give up a run to get an out. But no ground ball is forthcoming—Griffey powders the ball to left center, sending Lynn back, back to the wall. He leaps . . . and he and the ball hit the wall together. As the ball bounds away, Lynn crashes with a sickening thud that resounds throughout Fenway Park. As he crumples to the warning track two Reds score, and Griffey steams into third. Time is called. Lynn still has not moved.

Players spill out of the dugout and rush to his aid. The crowd is hushed, wondering if he is unconscious, wondering how many bones are broken, when Fred picks himself up, shakes out the bruises, and resumes his station in center field. Incredible!

After the delay, the Reds pick up where they left off. Bench leans on a curveball and lines a single off the wall in left; the score is tied. Though Tiant fans his countryman Tony Perez to end the fifth, the momentum has clearly shifted to the Reds.

The fourth pitcher for Cincinnati now enters the game— right-hander Clay Carroll, a veteran fireman and holder of

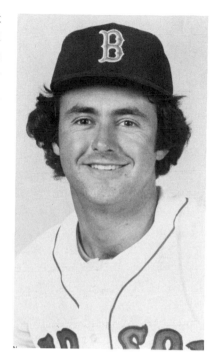

Fred Lynn

the National League record for saves in a season. After an inning-opening one-base hit by Yaz, he sets down the Sox easily. However, he does not come back to pitch the sixth, for the Reds mount a minor flurry against Tiant in the top of the frame and Carroll is pulled for a pinch batter. Tiant manages to hold the Reds off the scoreboard, but clearly is not the baffling *señor* of the early innings.

Captain Hook is in high gear tonight: In comes Pedro Borbon, a curveballing righty, to become the fifth Cincinnati pitcher in six innings. Three Sox up, three Sox down. The bullpen is doing the job, just as it has all season long.

Looie is not so economical. Griffey starts the Red seventh with a bouncing single to right, and goes to second when Morgan drops another single into left. Anderson, were he managing the Sox, would have Tiant out of the game right now, if he had not yanked him earlier—provided, that is, he could call on the Cincinnati relief corps. Darrell Johnson does not have a "stopper" in his bullpen, though Jim Willoughby and Dick Drago have both been reasonably effective, so he must stick with his starters perhaps a little longer than he would like to. Besides, great pitchers like Tiant can dig down deep for that "something extra" when they get in a jam, and reward the patient manager.

Tiant digs down deep and gets Bench on a fly to left, though Yaz backs to the wall to make the grab. Next he retires Perez on a fly to right, on which Griffey tags and moves to third. But as Looie digs down deep and then deeper, he suddenly touches bottom: There's nothing left. Foster pounds the ball off the center-field wall for a double, scoring Griffey and Morgan. Still no move to the bullpen. Concepcion grounds to short, and the dispirited Red Sox come in from the field, trailing by two.

And almost immediately, out they go to the field still trailing by two: Borbon has it easy with the limp Sox, getting three infield outs. Oh, well, many are thinking now, it's been a grand season in the home of the bean and the cod, and the Sox weren't expected to get this far anyway—Boston hasn't won a World Series since 1918, so why be disappointed if they don't win tonight?

Like a punch-drunk fighter trying to go the distance as a point of honor, Tiant comes out for the eighth round. And the Reds' first blow is a zinger, as Geronimo, the "out" in the Cincy batting order, hits a home run to right. Tiant is gone now, knocked out at last. Johnson takes the ball from his ace, who leaves to thunderous and well-deserved acclaim, and hands it to Roger Moret. A matchstick-thin left-hander with great stuff, Moret has seen only one-third of an inning's work in the Series despite his 14–3 season's mark. Roger zips through three batters handily: Borbon—Sparky let him bat!—Rose, and Griffey.

Perhaps Captain Hook was too kindhearted for once. Lynn opens the Boston eighth with a single off Borbon's leg, and Petrocelli extracts a base on balls. Kicking himself, no doubt, Anderson comes out to remove Pete and bring in his sixth hurler of the evening, Rawlins Jackson Eastwick III. A rookie who didn't come up to the big club until May 20, the twenty-four-year-old right-hander with the aristocratic name led all National League firemen in saves. In the Series he has been nothing short of magnificent, winning two games and saving another.

Rawly sets to work, striking out Dwight Evans and nailing Burleson on a fly to Foster. With Moret the scheduled batter, Johnson looks down his bench and reaches for Bernie Carbo, one-time Rookie of the Year with the Reds. Though he never lived up to the promise he showed in his first campaign, Bernie was a valuable reserve for the Red Sox this year and contributed a pinch-hit homer in Game Three. Could he possibly do it again?

Eastwick gets two quick strikes, then goes for the strikeout with a wicked slider inside. Carbo, completely fooled, takes a puny, dreadful-looking swing and barely flicks the ball foul. But the next pitch he drives high and far into the center-field bleachers, tying the game, and the 35,205 in Fenway shoot out of their seats as if they have been electrified. The jubilant fans, so recently beyond a glimmer of hope, continue to yell themselves hoarse as Cecil Cooper fans to end the eighth.

The new Boston pitcher is Dick Drago, who led Boston's bullpen this year with 15 saves and was a star of the Championship Series with Oakland. As Dick takes the mound, Carbo goes to left field, and Yaz replaces Cooper at first; the move is designed to put Drago in Cooper's leadoff spot and thus a maxi-

Bernie Carbo powers Rawly Eastwick's pitch into the center-field bleachers. Should Captain Hook have brought in Will McEnaney to face Carbo?

mum eight places away from having to bat, and also to play the hot hand, Carbo. Drago, primarily a fastball pitcher, blows the Reds away in the ninth, getting Morgan and Perez on foul pops to first and Bench on a grounder to third. Remember that "momentum" I mentioned a few innings back? It's shifted again.

Denny Doyle walks to lead off the bottom of the ninth. Next up is Carl Yastrzemski, coming off an injury-plagued year which saw him produce the lowest RBI total of his career. Still, in the clutch, who would you rather have up there than Yaz? He justifies the faith of the fans by driving a hard single to right that sends Doyle scampering to third. No one out—chalk one up in the win column, right? Not quite yet.

Will McEnaney relieves Eastwick. Southpaw McEnaney, though a twenty-three-year-old rookie, is cool enough to perform even under this kind of pressure. As he did back in the third inning, Anderson orders an intentional pass to Fisk. McEnaney gets Lynn on a shallow fly to Foster in foul ground—but uh-oh, here comes Doyle, determined to score after the catch despite the "hold" sign of the third-base coach. Foster does not throw particularly well, but Lynn's ball is so short that George nails Doyle at the plate by plenty. Petrocelli grounds out, and we go to overtime.

Foster grounds to Burleson as the first man up in the tenth, then Concepcion follows with a single to center. Davey is the first Red to reach base since Tiant left and took his pickoff move with him. Drago tries to hold the runner close, but with Geronimo at the plate, Concepcion takes off for second and steals it cleanly. Now *that's* out of the way, Drago thinks, and turns back to home, mowing down Geronimo on strikes and getting pinch hitter Dan Driessen on a fly to Carbo.

That pinch hitter means an eighth Cincinnati pitcher, tying a Series record; Anderson calls for Pat Darcy, yet another rookie who made it big this year. Employed mostly as a starter, the cocky right-hander was 2–5 in midseason, then won his last nine. Facing Evans, Burleson, and Carbo, he does not allow a ball out of the infield, and it's on to the eleventh. Is Boston's only hope that the Reds run out of pitchers? Except for tomorrow's scheduled starter, Don Gullett, only one hurler remains in the pen.

Drago immediately puts himself in hot water by hitting Rose with a pitch. The book calls for a sacrifice in this situation, and Griffey lays one down. Fisk, however, makes an exceptional play, pouncing on the bunt and forcing Rose at second. But the Reds' failure to move a man up suddenly seems not to matter anymore when Joe Morgan clobbers a ball to deep right. As the ball leaves the bat everyone in the park is certain it's a home run. Dwight Evans chases after it despite thinking to himself, "I haven't got a chance." But look at the ball, as it darts by us and heads for the stands—it is hit hard enough to be a homer, but is it high enough to carry all the way? There—the top spin on the ball is beginning to make it sink, yet still it looks as if it will fall in the warning track for a double or triple. With his back to the infield, running at full tilt toward the wall, Evans leaps, extends his glove hand as far as it will go, lunges at the last moment . . . and makes the catch! Not pausing to reflect on the miracle he has just accomplished, Evans instantly whirls and heaves the ball to first base, doubling up the amazed Griffey, who was nearly at third when Evans made the grab.

It is a phenomenal catch, ranking with such World Series greats as the catch Al Gionfriddo made in 1947, the one Willie Mays made in 1954, and the one Ron Swoboda made in 1969. Pete Rose, after the game, will say, "If he makes catches like that all the time I don't ever want to hit one to right. . . . It was like he had magnets in his glove." Sparky Anderson will call it simply "the greatest catch I've ever seen."

You'd think the boys from Beantown would be pretty revved

up by that catch, and would go out and grab the victory. But no, the Red Sox batters go down like tin soldiers, and the game, nearing four hours old now, goes on.

Rick Miller had pinch-hit for Drago in the eleventh, and now Rick Wise takes the hill for Boston. A veteran starter whose 19–12 record was the team's best, Wise has not pitched in relief since 1973; in the last eight years he has made 245 starts against only 5 jaunts from the bullpen. A hard thrower who goes after hitters high in the strike zone, Rick also has a tendency to give up the long ball. And he was bombed for five runs in four and a third innings as the starter in Game Three. It is time for Boston fans to get nervous if they are not so already.

Johnny Bench is Wise's first batter; he lifts a foul toward the stands between home and third. Fisk locates the ball, then runs to the wall. When he gets there, he looks up to regain sight of the ball, leans into the spectators, and makes a fine grab. Tony Perez follows with a single up the middle, then lumbers into second as Foster's blooper drops into shallow left. But here Wise draws the line: he induces Concepcion to fly out softly to Evans and whiffs Geronimo.

Due up for the Sox in what has become a battle of the bull-pens are Carlton Fisk, Fred Lynn, and Rico Petrocelli. Fisk steps in to try to get something started, and on the first pitch, a curve just below the waist, sends the ball into orbit up the left-field line. There's no doubt that it's long enough and high enough to go out; but will it be a fair ball? Urged on by everyone in the park, the ball sails above the height of the stadium, above the lights. Fisk stands a few steps from home, contorting his body and waving his arms in an attempt to direct the flight of the ball. Where this rock-jawed New Hampshire man learned to writhe like a witch doctor I don't know, but it works: The ball kisses the foul-pole screen as it descends, and at thirty-three minutes after midnight, the war is over.

Body English does the trick. Carlton Fisk's high drive to left field strikes the foul-pole screen, and the Red Sox obtain a last-minute stay of execution.

Red Sox players and patrons spill onto the field to greet Fisk at the end of his triumphal tour of the bases. The park's organist whips into an inspiring rendition of Handel's "Hallelujah Chorus," and all is right with the world. The sun will rise over Boston tomorrow, and the moon will glow over a baseball game in Fenway Park one more time.

Was that the greatest game ever played, or at least the greatest World Series game? What do you think? It's hard to rate the games, isn't it? It may be hard, and it is certainly unfair, but it's fun to try. Let's watch one last game, then compare our rankings and perhaps argue a bit.

October 21, 1975

CINCINNATI

	AB	R	H	P	A	E
Rose, 3b.	5	1	2	0	2	0
Griffey, rf.	5	2	2	0	0	0
Morgan, 2b.	6	1	1	5	3	0
Bench, c.	6	0	1	8	0	0
Perez, 1b.	6	0	2	10	3	0
Foster, lf.	6	0	2	4	1	0
Concepcion, ss.	6	0	1	3	4	0
Geronimo, cf.	6	1	2	2	0	0
Nolan, p.	0	0	0	1	0	0
a Chaney	1	0	0	0	0	0
Norman, p.	0	0	0	0	0	0
Billingham, p.	0	0	0	0	0	0
b Armbrister	0	1	0	0	0	0
Carroll, p.	0	0	0	0	0	0
c Crowley	1	0	1	0	0	0
Borbon, p.	1	0	0	0	0	0
Eastwick, p.	0	0	0	0	0	0
McEnaney, p.	0	0	0	0	0	0
e Driessen	1	0	0	0	0	0
Darcy, p.	0	0	0	0	1	0
TOTALS	50	6	14	33	14	0

BOSTON

	AB	R	H	P	A	E
Cooper, 1b.	5	0	0	8	0	0
Drago, p.	0	0	0	0	0	0
f Miller	1	0	0	0	0	0
Wise, p.	0	0	0	0	0	0
Doyle, 2b.	5	0	1	0	2	0
Yastrzemski, lf.-1b..	6	1	3	7	1	0
Fisk, c.	4	2	2	9	1	0
Lynn, cf.	4	2	2	2	0	0
Petrocelli, 3b.	4	1	0	1	1	0
Evans, rf.	5	0	1	3	1	0
Burleson, ss.	3	0	0	5	2	1
Tiant, p.	2	0	0	0	2	0
Moret, p.	0	0	0	0	1	0
d Carbo, lf.	2	1	1	1	0	0
TOTALS	41	7	10	36	11	1

a Flied out for Nolan in 3rd
b Walked for Billingham in 5th
c Singled for Carroll in 6th
d Homered for Moret in 8th
e Flied out for McEnaney in 10th
f Flied out for Drago in 11th

```
CINCINNATI    000   030   210   000 — 6
BOSTON        300   000   030   001 — 7
```

RBI—Griffey 2, Bench, Foster 2, Geronimo, Lynn 3, Carbo 3, Fisk. 2B—Doyle, Evans, Foster. 3B—Griffey. HR—Lynn, Geronimo, Carbo, Fisk. SB—Concepcion. Sac.—Tiant. DP—Cin. 1, Bos. 1. LOB—Cin. 11, Bos. 9. Umpires—Davidson, Frantz, Colosi, Barnett, Stello, Maloney. Time—4:01. Att.—35,205.

CINCINNATI	IP	H	R	ER	BB	SO
Nolan	2	3	3	3	0	2
Norman	⅔	1	0	0	2	0
Billingham	1⅓	1	0	0	1	1
Carroll	1	1	0	0	0	0
**Borbon	2	1	2	2	2	1
Eastwick	1⅓	2	1	1	1	2
McEnaney	⅔	0	0	0	1	0
***Darcy (L)	2	1	1	1	0	1
BOSTON						
*Tiant	7	11	6	6	2	5
Moret	1	0	0	0	0	0
Drago	3	1	0	0	0	1
Wise (W)	1	2	0	0	0	1

*Pitched to one batter in 8th
**Pitched to two batters in 8th
***Pitched to one batter in 12th
HBP—Drago (1)

October 2, 1978
New York Yankees
vs.
Boston Red Sox

The Red Sox went on to lose that World Series after all, though
the final game was tied with two out in the ninth. In defeat they
won the hearts of America, but the Reds got to wear the rings.
In the long New England winter that followed, talk about the
Sox was filled with "would'ves" and "could'ves" and "should'ves,"
a tradition dating back to 1920 when owner Harry Frazee,
strapped for cash, sold to the Yankees a young man named Ruth.

While the Yankees were building a dynasty, aided immeasur-
ably by the pitchers Boston gave them—Hall-of-Famers Herb
Pennock, Waite Hoyt, and Red Ruffing—Boston became the
doormat of the American League. Even after the franchise was

restored to health in the 1940s, there were still disappointments—final-day reversals which cost them the pennant in 1948 and 1949, and seventh-game losses in the World Series of 1946, 1967, and 1975.

After their thrilling but ultimately disappointing '75 season, the Red Sox stepped aside as their archrivals from New York, building a new dynasty with George Steinbrenner's millions, captured the American League flag the next two years. Then one month after the Yankees won the 1977 World Series, the Red Sox turned the tables of history and signed away the Yanks' postseason pitching hero, Mike Torrez. When they went on to deal for Cleveland's ace hurler, Dennis Eckersley, and California's fine second baseman, Jerry Remy, 1978 began to look like Boston's year.

And so it started out, as manager Don Zimmer's Red Sox took first place in the third week of May and didn't look back. On the morning of July 19, with an imposing record of 61–28, they led the second-place Milwaukee Brewers by eight games. The Yankees? They were buried in fourth place, fourteen games out and feuding. In the last game they had played, Reggie Jackson refused to obey manager Billy Martin's order to swing away and instead bunted foul into a strikeout. Furious, Martin suspended Jackson for flouting his authority. Scarcely noticed was the insubordination of fireman Sparky Lyle earlier in that game, when, after being called in to pitch in the fifth inning, he refused to come out of the dugout in the seventh. The Cy Young Award winner the previous year, Lyle was upset about being used in the middle innings only to give way to the newly acquired Goose Gossage, who would get credit for the save or the win. The champions were coming apart at the seams.

Billy Martin was on the way out right then, and though the Yanks rallied to win their next five games, he was forced to resign on July 24. Bob Lemon took his place and calmed the troubled waters, some injured players returned to active duty, and the Yanks started to win. And as they started to win, Boston started to lose. By July 31, the fourteen-game lead had been shaved to six and a half. But there the slide stopped—the Sox straightened themselves out and lost no more ground in August.

Then September came, and there was bleeding in Boston. While the Sox were losing fourteen of seventeen games, the Yankees were on a tear, taking fifteen of sixteen. In the midst of those opposing streaks the New Yorkers came into Fenway, where they had won the grand total of two games in two years, and staged a Boston Massacre scarcely less savage than the one in 1770. Four games out of first place at the time, the Yankees won all four games from Boston, leaving Fenway tied for the lead. The scores of the contests were 15–3, 13–2, 7–0, and 7–4; the Sox were outscored 42–9, outhit 67–21, and made 12 errors. This was beginning to look like the sorriest collapse since the Dodgers waved good-bye to a thirteen-and-a-half-game lead in six weeks of 1951.

The slide was dizzying: By September 16 the once mighty Red Sox were three and a half games out of first and sinking toward third place. But, miraculously, they revived. Winning eight in a row and twelve of their last fourteen, they pulled back into a tie on the final day of the season, as Tiant shut out Toronto while the Yankees were being blitzed by Cleveland. The Boston rally back from the brink was as amazing as the Yankees' stretch run; never had there been such a pennant race.

And thus we are here on this brilliantly sunny Monday in October, about to witness a one-game play-off for the title in the American League East. Only once before has there been a play-off in the junior circuit—thirty years ago, in this same park. Boston lost.

You'll recognize several of the men taking the field for Boston from the 1975 game: Over in left, Carl Yastrzemski, now thirty-

The most destructive right-handed batter in the American League in forty years, Jim Rice will be named Most Valuable Player in the off-season, beating out the Yankees' Ron Guidry.

nine but still a great player; in center, Fred Lynn, held back by injuries since his rookie season and not yet the player he was then (though he will regain his form in '79); at shortstop, Rick Burleson, a vastly improved player; and catching, Carlton Fisk, concluding a workhorse year which saw him behind the plate in 154 games.

But other faces are new: Second baseman Remy has solidified the defense, hit a respectable .278, and given Boston its first base-stealing threat in years. Third baseman Jack Brohamer, a utility infielder, is playing this afternoon because Butch Hobson, the regular third sacker, has bone chips in his elbow and cannot throw. In fact, Hobson has not been able to throw all season long, making 43 errors at third before coming to manager Don Zimmer ten days ago and asking out of the lineup. Butch, another in the long line of Boston's right-handed home-run heavies, will serve as the designated hitter today. At first base is a face both old and new, George Scott, who played there for the 1967 Red Sox, was traded to Milwaukee in 1971, and came back to Boston last year with Bernie Carbo in exchange for Cecil Cooper. After a tremendous return engagement in 1977, the big Boomer put on a lot of weight and tailed off badly at the plate.

In right field, where Dwight Evans played until he was beaned last month, is Jim Rice. An awesome right-handed slugger, he has led the American League in homers the last two seasons, and this time around added laurels for most RBI's, most hits, and most total bases. After today, his 1978 line will read: .315 average, 213 hits, 121 runs, 25 doubles, 15 triples, 46 homers, 139 RBI's, and 406 total bases (the highest figure in the American League since Joe DiMaggio's in 1937).

And on the mound, fittingly, is Mike Torrez, the burly right-hander who left New York to sign a seven-year pact with the Red Sox worth more than 2.5 million dollars. The Yankees did not lack the money to equal Boston's bid, for they later gave even more to get Gossage. They simply felt that at thirty-two

Torrez, who relies primarily on the fastball, would soon slip, and wasn't worth locking up for a long-term contract. Mike would like nothing better than to prove the Yankees wrong. The Yankees, on the other hand, would like nothing better than to beat Torrez, whom they accuse of bad-mouthing them to the press.

The first man Torrez will face in today's classic showdown is Mickey Rivers. This lithe whippet has lost more than sixty points from his .326 batting average of last year; but in 1978 he has played far better for Lemon than he did for Martin. Mick the Quick walks on four pitches and, on the first pitch to Thurman Munson, steals second. The crowd is still, taken aback by this sudden aggression.

Like Rivers, Munson has had an off year; a bad hand has robbed him of his power and consequently, though his average has held up pretty well, his home runs and RBI's have dropped off dramatically. With Rivers dancing off second to unnerve Torrez, the big guy—6'5", 220 pounds—shows what he's made of, fanning the Yankee catcher. Next he disposes of Lou Piniella, a .315 hitter, on a grounder to third. Up to the plate marches Reggie Jackson, "Mr. October," whose three home runs in the final game of the 1977 Series combined with Torrez's moundwork to defeat the Dodgers. Mike fires; Reggie swings: The ball sails high and deep to left. On another day, this would be a classic lob over The Green Monster—but today the wind is blowing briskly from left to right, and the ball descends to the warning track, where Yaz gloves it to end the top half of the inning.

Now let's have a look at the team that, win or lose, has already taken its place in history beside the 1914 Braves, the 1935 Cubs, the 1942 Cards, and the 1951 Giants. At third is Graig Nettles, the best at his position since the retirement of Brooks Robinson and a left-handed belter who can be counted on to knock out twenty-five to thirty homers and drive in ninety to a hundred runs a year. The shortstop is Bucky Dent, in his second year with New York since coming over from the White Sox. Only a .243 hitter, in the field Bucky is dependable rather than flashy—he may not make the great plays, but he won't kick the ones he ought to make. At second we see Brian Doyle, a frail-looking rookie with only fifty big-league at bats under his belt; he plays today in place of injured Willie Randolph. The first baseman is steady Chris Chambliss, who once again has driven in his ninety runs and played almost flawlessly in the field.

In right is Lou Piniella, who at age thirty-five doesn't cover a lot of ground but doesn't make any mistakes. He's a lifetime .290 hitter who is best described with the same adjectives which fit so many of these Yankees—steady, dependable, reliable. Across the outfield in left is yet another who is cut from this mold: thirty-four-year-old Roy White, little used by Martin but restored to his left-field post by Lemon and a key factor in the great stretch run. White does everything well except throw, and because his shortcoming is shared by Rivers in center, the Yankees can be victimized by aggressive baserunning. Rivers is a real rabbit, though, and covers so much ground that, on balance, his defense must be rated a plus. The designated hitter, under protest, is Reggie Jackson, who feels he ought to be playing right field; though he has played it well in seasons past, both last year and this his glovework has left a lot to be desired.

Another Yankee not blessed with a strong throwing arm is Munson, but he has learned to compensate by releasing his throws to second base more quickly than any receiver in the game. With a bat in his hand, he has been one of baseball's best clutch hitters, a star in postseason competition, and the MVP in the American League in 1976.

His battery mate is Ron Guidry, the Louisiana Cajun who is completing one of the best seasons any pitcher has ever had. Going into today's game his record is an unbelievable 24–3, and if he does not absorb a loss he will finish with the highest winning percentage of any 20-game winner in major-league history. His earned-run average is under 1.75, he has hurled nine shutouts, and in a game against the Angels he fanned 18. Today, however, he is pitching with only three days' rest; he is accustomed to four. Will this skinny left-hander have his fastball?

The answer seems to be yes, as he fans Burleson and Rice while retiring the side in order in the first. But in fact, the pitch Guidry used to strike them out with was his hard slider, which transformed him from a marginal big-league hurler to the best there is. Ron learned the slider from Sparky Lyle, and he throws it as hard as he does his fastball. It is nearly impossible for a batter to tell which pitch is coming at him until it is too late to adjust for the break.

Torrez also looks sharp as he zips through Nettles, Chambliss, and White, all left-handed batters (White is actually a switch-hitter). He, too, is throwing many more sliders thus far than he customarily does. Despite their devastating batwork in September's Boston Massacre, the predominantly left-handed Yankees are at a distinct disadvantage in Fenway, where any right-handed hitter is a home-run threat. For this same reason, most managers are reluctant to start a left-handed hurler here. Guidry, though, is the exception: He's just so good that the percentages are thrown out the window. If it's his day to pitch, he pitches.

Batting for Boston now is left-handed Yastrzemski, who shows what he thinks of the percentages by ripping the second pitch thrown to him down the line in right for a home run. The stadium rocks with applause for their long-time star, an autumn hero once again. Optimistic cheers greet Fisk, Lynn, and Hobson as they follow to the plate, but Guidry quiets the crowd by disposing of them in order. Almost unnoticed is the fact that the wind has just shifted. Any fly ball hit out to The Monster now will get a little boost.

After Doyle and Dent go down to open the third, Rivers reaches Torrez for the first Yankee hit—a grounder drilled up

Ron Guidry's dazzling 1978 campaign bears comparison with the legendary pitching achievements of all time. The mystery is how a 5'10", 160-pound stringbean can throw the ball at 98 miles per hour.

the right-field line for a double. As he did in the first, Torrez feeds Munson pitch after pitch on the outside of the plate. Ordinarily this is just where Thurman likes the ball, but today it seems he wants to pull. While chasing a pitch in the dirt he fans once again. By offering such temptation, The Green Monster probably harms more right-handed hitters than it helps.

George Scott leads off the Boston third with a tremendous blast to center. Look at Rivers drifting back on the ball—he doesn't know where it is! He has forgotten to clip his sunglasses on between innings, and now it is too late; the sun is blazing at full force, and the ball, which Mickey might have reached with a good start, falls to earth at the base of the center-field wall. The Boomer pulls into second with a double. Jack Brohamer, a .235 hitter before today, follows with a neat sacrifice bunt to third, advancing Scott. Burleson comes to the plate, hoping to drive one to the outfield and put Boston up by two. Guidry throws him a hard slider down and in, however, and Rooster taps the ball to Nettles at third. Scott has no choice but to hold, and the throw goes across the diamond for the out. Remy flies to left, and the rally fizzles.

Surprisingly, Torrez continues to rely on his glider and an occasional curve rather than the fastball, which he seems unable to keep down in the strike zone. He holds New York in check in the fourth, despite a leadoff single by Piniella and a vicious liner to right by Jackson. Guidry keeps pace in the bottom half, knocking off the heart of the Sox order—Rice, Yaz, and Fisk—but he is relying almost exclusively now on the slider, a tremendous strain on his arm.

Though he has the distressing habit of falling behind in the count, Torrez has tremendous stuff: Pitching in the classic Fenway pattern—up and in to the lefties and down and away to the righties—he is showing his consciousness of The Wall. Roy White extracts a walk from Big Mike to open the New York fifth, but Doyle, Dent, and Rivers fail to bring him around. Interestingly, Dent is the only one of New York's three right-handed batters whom Torrez has pitched high and inside—but Mike can hardly be called foolhardy for daring to challenge a ninth-place hitter with only four homers.

An infield single to Hobson provides the only flicker of offense for Boston in their half of the fifth, and then Torrez sets to work again. He fans Munson for the third time, gets Piniella on a fly to Lynn in fairly deep center, and induces Reggie to bounce to Remy. Torrez won his last start 1–0 over Detroit right here in Fenway. Will lightning strike twice?

Burleson, who stranded Scott at third in his last trip, leads off the sixth with a ringing double to the left-field corner. Once again, manager Zimmer plays for one run and has Remy bunt Rooster over to third. Now, with Jim Rice up, we have a classic confrontation: baseball's best hitter versus its best pitcher. And this time Rice wins the skirmish, singling to center to put his team up by two. After Jim advances to second as Yaz grounds out, Guidry elects to put Fisk on deliberately and pitch to Lynn. Fred sends a vicious liner to deep right field, just a few feet to the left of the foul line—a place, Lynn is later to say, where "I don't hit five balls all season." Yet Piniella is positioned over toward the line, and though he loses sight of the ball in the sun momentarily, he is able to race to his left, respot the ball, and seize it just one stride from the stands. Had the ball not been caught, the score would now be 4–0. Why was Piniella playing Lynn as a dead pull hitter? After the game, Lou will confess he doesn't know; maybe he made a mistake.

Torrez retires Nettles as we enter the last third of the game, then sees Chambliss dribble an outside pitch between short and third—only the third Yankee hit this afternoon. Roy White follows with a well-hit single to center, and it's time for Lemon to make a move: The next two batters are Doyle and Dent, but he has only one infield reserve on the bench and cannot pinch-hit for both of them. Lemon chooses to go for the power hitter

Bucky Dent, the man of the hour. Listen to Mike Torrez's account: "I thought I jammed him enough. I was so damned shocked when it went out. I thought it was just a fly ball off the wall. Then, 'Oh, my God!'"

right away, sending up Jim Spencer in Doyle's place (Fred Stanley will replace Doyle at second). Torrez still has his stuff; keeping the ball on the outside, he gets the dangerous left-handed batter on a fly to left.

Now the batter is Dent, 0–for–2 to this point. Young, handsome, and talented, Bucky was having a splendid season till the Yankees caught Boston; then his average began to plummet. Just last night, owner George Steinbrenner called Bucky over and showed him a piece of paper which proved that over the previous twenty games or so he'd been hitting .140. "Don't let that discourage you," Steinbrenner said. "You're overdue and you'll snap out of it."

After taking a pitch for a ball, Dent swings at an inside fast-ball and fouls it straight down onto his left ankle, the one he has struck so often in the past. Bucky has been wearing a protective device at the plate, but abandoned it for today's game. The flash of pain is overwhelming. He falls to the ground, then scrambles back up and hobbles around trying to shake off the ache. Meanwhile, in the on-deck circle, Mickey Rivers hands the batboy a new bat (the Roy White model that Rivers and Dent use). "Give this to Bucky," Mick says. "There's a home run in it." The batboy follows orders and Dent, not giving a thought to which bat he brings to the plate, accepts the new one. The next pitch is a fastball, inside and up. Dent jerks back from the plate slightly and punches at the ball, sending it soaring to left.

Torrez instantly knows he's made a mistake, but he thinks the ball will be caught at the wall or at worst rebound off it. In left, Yastrzemski doesn't think the ball has enough carry to go out, and plants himself at the base of the wall to make the catch. Dent, running to first, does think the ball will strike the wall. Then rounding first, he hears the groan of the crowd and looks up to see the ball clear the fence by the barest of margins and settle into the screen. The Yanks take the lead! The Red Sox and their rooters cannot believe it. A homer from Jackson, or

Nettles, or Chambliss, or Munson, or anybody in the Yankee lineup—that could be understood in a game of this importance. But Bucky Dent?

Has Torrez suddenly wilted? Or was Dent's homer a freak blow from which he can recover? Mickey Rivers, the man behind the scenes a moment ago, now takes his turn at the plate. Pitching carefully, Torrez runs the count out to 3–2, then, as he did in the first, puts Rivers on. And as Rivers did in the first, he steals to put himself in scoring position. Will Zimmer leave Torrez in to try to fan Munson once more? No. Out goes Torrez and in comes Bob Stanley, a sinkerball pitcher whose record is 15–2. Munson greets him with a looping double into left center which scores Rivers easily. Stanley then gets Piniella, and the game is still within reach.

After Guidry retires Hobson, George Scott singles to stir up a little enthusiasm. But Bob Lemon acts swiftly to dampen any hopes the Sox might be entertaining. He takes the ball from Guidry, who has had to struggle all game long to compensate for the lack of his fastball, and hands it to Rich Gossage, a heavy-set right-hander who, if anything, is faster than Guidry. In his first year as a Yankee, the Goose has been the league's top fireman, and is the man responsible for Sparky Lyle's overnight descent "from Cy Young to sayonara," in Graig Nettles's quip. Gossage makes short work of pinch-hitter Bob Bailey, batting for Brohamer, and Rick Burleson, and the Yanks are six outs away from the flag.

Leading off the top of the eighth is Reggie Jackson, who crunches a belt-high fastball 430 feet into the bleachers in right center. As he trots around the bases, he thinks to himself, "It's just another run." With Chambliss and Nettles to follow, Zimmer calls for a left-hander, Andy Hassler, who does the job. Now all Boston has to do is score three runs off the top reliever in the American League.

Gossage's delivery is just the opposite of Guidry's: Where

Reggie Jackson, Mr. October, does it again. His reputation was earned largely in the 1977 World Series, when he hit a record five home runs—three of them coming on three consecutive pitches in the final game.

Ron whistled the ball up to the plate with a compact, easy motion that made his speed all the more deceptive, Goose puts everything he's got into each pitch, rocking back, flipping his left foot out and muscling the ball to the plate. His fastball moves more than Guidry's, so he doesn't try to spot it: He just directs it toward the plate and lets it sail or dip as it will. He throws a dynamite pitch to Jerry Remy, leading off the eighth—a fastball that plummets at the last moment from the knees to the ground; but Remy reaches down and whacks it for a double. Rice cannot come through, but Yaz can, singling to center and bringing Remy home. Goose gets two strikes on Carlton Fisk, but cannot get the third. After fouling off four two-strike pitches to the *oohs* and *ahs* of the crowd, Fisk drives another single to center, sending Yaz to second. Now the tying run is on base and the lead run comes to the plate in the person of Fred Lynn. When he singles to left to bring Yaz home, Fenway becomes a madhouse. The score is 5–4, Gossage is on the ropes, and victory, that faintest of hopes when the inning began, now seems almost assured. Men on first and second, one man out—who will Lemon bring in from the bullpen? Perhaps Lyle, last year's hero? No . . . he's going to stick with his best: Gossage stays in. And as quickly as the euphoria of the crowd mounted, as quickly it vanishes, for Hobson flies to right and Scott, to a smattering of boos, strikes out. While not a soul is getting up to leave, many must feel that their team has just let opportunity go begging, and opportunity does not knock twice.

With two out in the top of the ninth, Lemon sends Paul Blair up to bat for Rivers. A defensive specialist who often caddies for Mickey in the late innings, Blair provides a bonus with an unexpected base hit (Blair was batting .169 at the time). With Munson due up next, Hassler gives way to right-handed Dick Drago. The move pays off, and the Sox head into the final turn still needing only one to tie.

First up in the ninth is Dwight Evans, hitting for third-baseman Frank Duffy, who replaced Brohamer in the eighth. Evans is still suffering dizzy spells from the beaning he took last month, but is evidently well enough to bat. A home run, or even a hit, would be a dramatic and satisfying end to this fine outfielder's ruined season; but Fate has not written him a happy part in this drama. He flies out, and the Sox are now down to two outs. Gossage, for whom control is sometimes a problem, sees it elude him with Burleson at the plate; Rooster walks, and the fans begin to cheer, to plead with Remy to get a hit. But all Jerry can do is send a mild line drive to medium right. Once again Piniella has positioned himself perfectly. He takes one step to his left . . . halts . . . drifts back another step; now he throws his arms out in despair . . . *he can't see the ball!*

But Lady Luck is with Lou and the Yankees today. Burleson, heading for second base, does not realize that Piniella hasn't a clue where the ball is, and he doesn't see third-base coach Eddie Yost excitedly waving him on to third. So he holds up to see if the ball will be caught. Miraculously, the liner drops right at Piniella's feet, then kicks up to his left. Lou flicks out his glove and makes the grab, much as a hockey goaltender would snare a slapshot. He fires the ball in to the cut-off man, and Burleson cannot advance beyond second. Jim Rice follows with a long fly to right that would have scored Burleson easily had he advanced to third on Remy's hit. As it is, Piniella makes the catch, Burleson tags up and goes to third, and Remy holds at first.

Now the season has come down to the ninety feet between Rick Burleson and home plate, and the sixty feet six inches between Goose Gossage and Carl Yastrzemski. The tension is unbearable. Yaz is the man you'd want to have at bat in this situation: First, he's a proven clutch performer whose powers of concentration can lift him above the pressure; second, he's a fastball hitter facing a fastball pitcher; and third, he's hit the ball hard this afternoon. Gossage will not experiment with a change of pace or a breaking pitch now, as he sometimes does to amuse himself. His philosophy is the traditional one of the relief pitcher who's in a do-or-die situation: If you're going to lose, let it be on your best pitch. For Gossage, of course, this means the fastball, which he will fire as hard as he can and not give a thought to location.

Yaz is thinking, too: He's not going to play long ball, but will simply look for something inside that he can drive through the hole between first and second. Chambliss holds Remy close to the bag, for he is the winning run and must be kept out of scoring position.

The first pitch to Yaz is off the plate, and he watches it sail by. Then his eyes light up—here comes the low inside fastball he'd been hoping to get. It is headed for the inside corner, knee-high; Yaz swings. Gossage's best fastballs, however, have a hop on them, and this pitch rises slightly as it nears the plate. Yaz hits under the ball and sends it high in the air over third base. The ball is drifting foul, but not far off the line. Nettles camps under it, squeezes it, and the Yankees have held on, putting a great finishing touch to the American League's greatest title drive.

Gossage leaps into the air, and the Yankees spill out of the dugout onto the field to form the joyous and familiar scene of winners exulting. The Red Sox? They trudge to the locker room in silence, some in tears, and brace themselves for the onslaught of the press. There will be questions for Mike Torrez about the home-run pitch, for Rick Burleson about his baserunning, for Carl Yastrzemski about the final pitch. But the question for which no one will have an answer is why, when two teams have battled so valiantly for so long, and in the end are separated by so little, one should have to lose.

October 2, 1978

NEW YORK	AB	R	H	P	A	E
Rivers, cf.	2	1	1	2	0	0
c. Blair, cf.	1	0	1	0	0	0
Munson, c.	5	0	1	7	1	0
Piniella, rf.	4	0	1	4	0	0
Jackson, dh.	4	1	1	0	0	0
Nettles, 3b.	4	0	0	1	3	0
Chambliss, 1b.	4	1	1	8	0	0
White, lf.	3	1	1	4	0	0
Thomasson, lf.	0	0	0	1	0	0
Doyle, 2b.	2	0	0	0	0	0
a Spencer	1	0	0	0	0	0
Stanley, 2b.	1	0	0	0	0	0
Dent, ss.	4	1	1	0	2	0
Guidry, p.	0	0	0	0	1	0
Gossage, p.	0	0	0	0	0	0
TOTALS	35	5	8	27	7	0

BOSTON	AB	R	H	P	A	E
Burleson, ss.	4	1	1	4	2	0
Remy, 2b.	4	1	2	2	5	0
Rice, rf.	5	0	1	4	0	0
Yastrzemski, lf. ...	5	2	2	2	0	0
Fisk, c.	3	0	1	5	1	0
Lynn, cf.	4	0	1	1	0	0
Hobson, dh.	4	0	1	0	0	0
Scott, 1b.	4	0	2	8	0	0
Brohamer, 3b.	1	0	0	1	1	0
b Bailey	1	0	0	0	0	0
Duffy, 3b.	0	0	0	0	0	0
d Evans	1	0	0	0	0	0
Torrez, p.	0	0	0	0	0	0
Stanley, p.	0	0	0	0	0	0
Hassler, p.	0	0	0	0	0	0
Drago, p.	0	0	0	0	0	0
TOTALS	36	4	11	27	9	0

a Flied out for Doyle in 7th
b Struck out for Brohamer in 7th
c Singled for Rivers in 9th
d Popped out for Duffy in 9th

```
NEW YORK    000  000  410 — 5
BOSTON      010  001  020 — 4
```

RBI—Dent 3, Munson, Jackson, Yastrzemski 2, Rice, Lynn. 2B—Rivers, Scott, Burleson, Munson, Remy. HR—Yastrzemski, Dent, Jackson. SB—Rivers 2. Sac.—Brohamer, Remy. PB—Munson. LOB—N.Y. 6, Bos., 9. Umpires—Denkinger, Evans, Clark, Palermo. Time—2:52. Att.—32,925.

NEW YORK	IP	H	R	ER	BB	SO
Guidry (W)	6⅓	6	2	2	1	5
Gossage (Save)	2⅔	5	2	2	1	2

BOSTON	IP	H	R	ER	BB	SO
Torrez (L)	6⅔	5	4	4	3	4
*Stanley	⅓	2	1	1	0	0
Hassler	1⅔	1	0	0	0	2
Drago	⅓	0	0	0	0	0

*Pitched to one batter in 8th

New York Yankees vs. Boston Red Sox

Afterword

Well, that 1978 game brings us up almost to the present day. Will another one come along to squeeze its way onto the Ten Greatest list? Certainly—that's what happened in 1978, in 1975, in 1960. . . . Though it may not come this year, or the next, or the one after that, it *will* come, and one of our ten greatest games will be displaced from the list.

Which one will be the first to drop off? To know that we must, at last, make a ranking of the games. Why don't you do yours first so we can compare? I'll offer mine on the next page.

If you'd like to tell me why your list makes more sense than mine, or if I've left off altogether a game *you* feel belongs among the ten greatest ever played, I'd be happy to hear from you: Write to me in care of the publisher, Four Winds Press, 50 West 44th Street, New York, New York 10036.

My ten greatest games, in order:

1. October 3, 1951—New York 5, Brooklyn 4.
2. October 13, 1960—Pittsburgh 10, New York 9.
3. October 10, 1924—Washington 4, New York 3.
4. October 21, 1975—Boston 7, Cincinnati 6.
5. October 8, 1956—New York 2, Brooklyn 0.
6. May 26, 1959—Milwaukee 1, Pittsburgh 0.
7. May 2, 1917—Cincinnati 1, Chicago 0.
8. September 30, 1907—Detroit 9, Philadelphia 9.
9. October 12, 1929—Philadelphia 10, Chicago 8.
10. October 2, 1978—New York 5, Boston 4.

And, for argument's sake, here are five more games which many people might have placed on the list:

October 2, 1908—Cleveland 1, Chicago (AL) 0; Addie Joss throws a perfect game to win while Ed Walsh strikes out 15 in defeat.

October 8, 1908—Chicago (NL) 4, New York (NL) 2; one-game play-off for pennant resulting from Merkle's "boner" two weeks earlier.

October 16, 1912—Boston (AL) 3, New York (NL) 2; Sox take final game of World Series with two runs in bottom of tenth inning.

October 3, 1947—Brooklyn 3, New York (AL) 2; on final pitch, Yank hurler Bill Bevens loses both no-hitter and game.

October 12, 1980—Philadelphia 8 (NL), Houston 7; 10 innings, the most dramatic finale of a championship series.

These are all great contests, as you can tell from even a one-sentence description—yet I believe that together we have seen ten that were even better. I hope you've enjoyed them.

Index

Aaron, Henry, 116, 120, 123, 125, 129–130
Adcock, Joe, 116, 117, 120, 123, 125, 128, 129–130
Alston, Walter, 99, 104, 106
Amoros, Sandy, 102, 106, 108
Anderson, Sparky, 155, 160, 161, 163, 166, 167
Armbrister, Ed, 160
Ashburn, Richie, 123

Bailey, Bob, 186
Baker, Del, 99
Barnes, Jesse, 48
Barnes, Virgil, 47, 48, 50, 53, 54
Bauer, Hank, 101, 102, 104, 106, 108
Bench, Johnny, 158, 159, 162, 166, 167
Bender, Chief, 8
Bentley, Jack, 47–48, 56–57
Berra, Yogi, 73, 98, 101, 104, 106, 107, 109, 112, 135–136, 139, 141, 143, 144, 146, 147–148
Bevens, Bill, 107
Billingham, Jack, 160
Bishop, Max, 65, 66, 70, 72
Blair, Paul, 188

Blake, Sheriff, 72–73
Blanchard, John, 136, 141, 142, 143, 146
Bluege, Ossie, 46, 51, 53, 55–56, 57
Boley, Joe, 65, 66, 67, 71, 72, 73
Borbon, Pedro, 161, 162, 163
Boston Braves, 66, 79
Boston Red Sox, 4, 99
    1975: 153–170, 194
    1978: 173–190, 194
Boyer, Clete, 84, 135, 141, 142, 144, 148
Branca, Ralph, 4, 89, 90, 91, 94, 97, 115, 150
Brecheen, Harry, 120
Bridges, Tommy, 109
Brohamer, Jack, 177, 182, 186, 189
Brooklyn Dodgers, 3, 116, 119, 175
    1951: 77–94, 194
    1956: 97–112, 194
Bruton, Billy, 117
Buhl, Bob, 116
Bunning, Jim, 123
Burdette, Lew, 116, 117, 118, 120, 122, 123, 124, 125, 128, 135
Burgess, Smokey, 119, 123, 125, 136–138, 139, 144

Burleson, Rick, 156, 160, 163, 166, 177, 180, 182, 183, 186, 189, 190
Burns, George, 71–72, 73
Bush, Guy, 62, 63

Campanella, Roy, 83, 102, 106, 109
Carbo, Bernie, 163, 164
Carey, Andy, 101, 102, 104, 106, 107, 108
Carroll, Clay, 161
Cerv, Bob, 135
Chambliss, Chris, 179, 180, 183, 186, 189
Chase, Hal, 31, 32, 34, 37, 38–39
Chicago Cubs, 103
  1917: 25–40, 194
  1929: 61–74, 194
Chicago Whales, 26
Chicago White Sox, 8
Christopher, Joe, 144
Cimoli, Gino, 135, 144, 145
Cincinnati Reds, 4
  1917: 25–40, 194
  1975: 153–170
Clemente, Roberto, 119, 136, 137, 141, 142, 145, 156
Cleveland Indians, 66
Cleveland "Naps," 8, 22
Coates, Jim, 145–146
Cobb, Ty, 5, 9, 12, 14, 16, 17–19, 20, 21, 22, 70
Cochrane, Mickey, 62, 64, 65, 66, 67, 68, 70, 72, 73, 74
Collins, Eddie, 22, 62, 63
Collins, Jimmy, 11, 12, 14, 16
Collins, Joe, 101, 102, 104, 106, 108
Columbia Park (Philadelphia), 7, 11, 61, 154
Comiskey Park (Chicago), 153
Concepcion, Dave, 158, 160, 162, 166, 168
Connolly, Tommy, 20
Coolidge, Calvin, 45, 46, 58
Cooper, Cecil, 156, 159, 160, 163
Coughlin, Bill, 12, 13, 16, 19
County Stadium (Milwaukee), 115, 116
Covington, Wes, 116, 120, 123, 128
Cox, Billy, 81, 83, 84, 85, 86, 91, 102
Crandall, Del, 117, 120, 123, 125, 128
Crawford, Sam, 12, 16, 17, 19, 20, 54
Crosley Field (Cincinnati), 154

Cross, Monte, 21
Cueto, Manny, 31, 32, 34, 36, 39
Cuyler, Kiki, 62, 65, 66, 67, 70

Darcy, Pat, 166–167
Dark, Alvin, 79–80, 83, 85, 88
Dascoli, Frank, 129–130
Davis, Harry, 11, 12, 13, 14, 18, 19, 20, 21, 22
Deal, Charlie, 27, 29, 32, 34, 36
DeMaestri, Joe, 145, 147
Dent, Bucky, 5, 178, 180, 182–183, 184, 185
Detroit Tigers, 7–22, 44, 61, 62, 194
DiMaggio, Joe, 100, 177
Donovan, "Wild Bill," 8, 9–10, 11, 12, 13, 14, 16, 19, 20, 21, 22
Doyle, Brian, 179, 180, 182, 185
Doyle, Denny, 156, 157, 160, 166
Doyle, Larry, 27, 29, 30, 32, 34, 35, 37, 39
Drago, Dick, 162, 163, 166, 167, 168, 188
Dressen, Charley, 83, 84, 85, 86, 88–89, 91, 97
Driessen, Dan, 166
Duffy, Frank, 189
Duren, Ryne, 135
Durocher, Leo, 78–79, 80, 86, 89, 91, 97
Dygert, Jimmy, 8, 10, 13, 22
Dykes, Jimmy, 65, 66, 67, 70, 71, 72, 73

Earnshaw, George, 62, 63
Eastwick, Rawly, 163, 166
Ebbets Field (Brooklyn), 99, 100, 154
Eckersley, Dennis, 79
Ehmke, Howard, 63
English, Woody, 65, 66, 70
Erskine, Carl, 89
Evans, Dwight, 156, 160, 163, 167, 168, 177, 189
Evers, Johnny, 31

Face, Roy, 138, 142, 143–144, 146
Fenway Park (Boston), 153–154, 160, 170, 175, 180, 182, 183, 188
Fisk, Carlton, 4, 156–157, 159, 160, 166, 167, 168–170, 175, 180, 182, 183, 188
Forbes Field (Pittsburgh), 139, 141, 143, 145, 154

Foster, George, 158, 159, 162, 163, 166, 168
Foxx, Jimmy, 62, 65, 66, 67, 71, 72, 73
Frazee, Harry, 173
Friend, Bob, 146–147
Frisch, Frankie, 46, 48, 50, 55, 56, 57
Furillo, Carl, 81, 83, 84, 86, 102, 108 109, 156

Gehrig, Lou, 62, 98, 103
Geronimo, Cesar, 158, 159, 160, 162, 166, 168
Getz, Gus, 35, 37
Gibbon, Joe, 147
Giles, Warren, 130
Gilliam, Jim ("Junior"), 101, 103, 107
Gionfriddo, Al, 167
Goslin, Goose, 46, 50, 53, 55, 57
Gossage, Rich ("Goose"), 17, 174, 177, 186, 188, 189–190
Gowdy, Hank, 48, 51, 53, 54, 56, 57
Griffey, Ken, 158, 160, 161–162, 163, 167
Griffith, Clark, 45, 47
Griffith Stadium (Washington, D.C.), 45
Grimm, Charley, 66, 67, 70, 74
Groat, Dick, 119, 134, 139, 141, 142, 144, 145, 147
Groh, Heinie, 29, 30, 32, 34, 35, 39, 46, 56
Grove, Lefty, 62, 63, 73–74
Guidry, Ron, 179–180, 181, 186
Gullett, Don, 167

Haas, Mule, 65, 66, 70, 72
Haddix, Harvey, 5, 115, 120, 122, 123– 125, 126, 128, 129, 130, 133, 138, 146, 147, 148
Haney, Fred, 117, 124, 129, 130
Harris, Bucky, 44, 45, 46, 47, 48, 50, 51, 53, 54, 55, 57, 58, 79, 101
Harris, Dave, 109
Hartnett, Gabby, 65
Hartsel, Topsy, 11, 12, 19
Hartung, Clint, 89
Hassler, Andy, 186, 188
Hearn, Jim, 79
Hoak, Don, 119, 120, 121, 123, 124, 128, 135, 139, 141, 143, 146
Hobson, Butch, 177, 180, 183, 186, 188

Hodges, Gil, 80, 81, 83, 86, 88, 99, 102, 104, 106, 108
Hogg, "Buffalo Bill," 9
Hornsby, Rogers, 62, 65, 66, 67, 70, 74
Howard, Elston, 135, 136
Hoyt, Waite, 173
Huhn, Hap, 31, 32, 36
Hunter, Jim ("Catfish"), 123

Irvin, Monte, 80, 81, 83, 85, 89

Jackson, Reggie, 4, 174, 178, 179, 182, 183, 185, 186, 187
Jackson, Travis, 48, 51, 56, 57
Jansen, Larry, 79, 88
Jennings, Hughie, 9, 10, 12, 13, 14, 16
Johnson, Darrell, 162, 163
Johnson, Walter, 5, 22, 44, 47, 54, 55, 56, 57
Jones, Davy, 11, 12, 13, 14, 16, 20
Joss, Addie, 123
Judge, Joe, 46, 48, 51, 55–56, 57

Kelly, George, 47, 48, 50–51, 53, 54, 55, 56
Killian, Ed, 21
Kiner, Ralph, 81
Kopf, Larry, 30, 32, 34, 35, 37, 38
Koslo, Dave, 79
Koufax, Sandy, 123
Kubek, Tony, 135, 136, 139, 141, 142, 143, 144–145
Kuhn, Bowie, 26

Lajoie, Napoleon, 8
Larsen, Don, 99–100, 101, 103, 106– 107, 108, 109, 112, 115, 123, 133, 138, 145
Law, Vernon, 138, 139, 141, 142, 146
Leibold, Nemo, 53, 54
Lemon, Bob, 174–175, 178, 179, 183, 186, 188
Lindstrom, Freddie, 46, 48, 51, 54, 56, 58
Lockman, Whitey, 80, 83, 84, 85, 89, 91
Logan, Johnny, 117, 120, 122, 124, 125, 128
Long, Dale, 147
Lopez, Hector, 135, 141
Los Angeles Dodgers, 4
Lyle, Sparky, 174, 180, 186, 188

Lynn, Fred, 154, 156, 159, 160–161, 163, 166, 168, 177, 180, 183, 188

McCarthy, Joe, 62, 72, 73
McDougald, Gil, 101, 102, 104, 107, 135, 147, 148
McEnaney, Will, 166
McGraw, John, 44, 47, 48, 50, 51, 54, 56, 57, 145
McIntire, Harry, 128
McMillan, Norm, 65, 66, 67, 70, 72
McNeely, Earl, 46, 48, 53–54, 55, 56, 57
McQuillan, Hugh, 56
McQuillen, George, 124
Mack, Connie (Cornelius McGillicuddy), 8, 9, 12, 13, 17, 19, 20, 62, 63, 71, 72
Maglie, Sal, 79, 81, 83, 84, 86, 88, 99, 101, 102, 104, 106, 107, 108
Malone, Pat, 62, 73, 74
Mann, Les, 27, 32, 34, 36
Mantilla, Felix, 128–129
Mantle, Mickey, 98, 100, 101, 102, 104, 105, 106, 107, 108, 136, 141, 142, 144, 147, 148
Marberry, Fred ("Firpo"), 44, 47, 51, 52, 53
Maris, Roger, 136, 139, 141, 142, 144, 145, 147
Martin, Billy, 101, 102–103, 104, 107, 108, 147, 174, 178, 179
Mathews, Eddie, 116, 117, 120, 122, 125, 129
Mathewson, Christy, 30, 31, 32, 34, 35
Mays, Willie, 80, 84, 85, 91, 167
Mazeroski, Bill, 119, 120, 124, 128, 134–135, 139, 141, 142, 144, 148–150
Meijas, Roman, 119, 120–122, 124
Merkle, Fred, 27, 29, 32, 34, 35, 37, 39
Meusel, Irish, 47, 50, 51, 54, 55, 57, 58
Miller, Bing, 65, 67, 71, 73
Miller, Ralph, 55, 56, 57
Miller, Rick, 168
Milwaukee Braves, 115–130, 194
Mitchell, Dale, 109, 112
Mitchell, Fred, 29, 32
Mizell, Vinegar Bend, 147
Mogridge, George, 46, 47, 48, 50, 51

Moret, Roger, 162–163
Morgan, Joe, 158, 162, 166, 167
Mueller, Don, 80, 83, 88–89
Munson, Thurman, 178, 179, 182, 183, 186
Murphy, Danny, 11, 12, 14, 16, 21
Murray, Bill, 124
Murtaugh, Danny, 115, 124, 128, 142, 143, 144, 146, 147–148

Neale, Greasy, 30, 31, 34, 35, 37
Negro Leagues, 80
Nehf, Art, 54, 56, 72
Nelson, Rocky, 119, 120, 122, 123, 128–129, 134, 139, 140, 141, 142, 145, 147–148
Nettles, Graig, 178, 180, 182–183, 186, 190
New York Giants, 3, 8, 27, 31, 65, 72
  1924: 43–58, 194
  1951: 77–94, 194
New York Highlanders. See also New York Yankees, 9, 17, 63
New York Yankees, 4, 78
  1956: 97–112, 116, 194
  1960: 133–150, 194
  1978: 173–190, 194
Newcombe, Don, 82, 83, 84, 85, 86, 88, 89
Nicholls, Simon, 11, 12, 16, 19
Noble, Ray, 88
no-hitters, 122, 123–125, 128, 129, 133
  double, 35–37
  in World Series, 97–112
Nolan, Gary, 159, 160
Norman, Fred, 160

Oakland A's, 155, 163
O'Brien, Eddie, 117
O'Brien, Johnny, 117, 120, 123, 125, 128
Ogden, Curly, 46
Oldring, Rube, 11, 13, 14, 16, 22
O'Leary, Charley, 12, 13, 14, 21
O'Loughlin, Silk, 14, 20
Orth, Al, 35, 39

Pafko, Andy, 81–83, 84, 86, 91, 117, 122, 124, 125, 128, 129
Payne, Fred, 16, 19
Peckinpaugh, Roger, 46
Pennock, Herb, 108, 173

Perez, Tony, 158, 161, 162, 166, 168
perfect games, 36
    Haddix's, 122, 123–125, 128,
        129, 133, 139, 146
    Larsen's, 97–112, 139
Perry, Gaylord, 117
Petrocelli, Rico, 156, 159, 160, 163,
    166, 168
Philadelphia A's
    1907: 7–22, 194
    1929: 61–74, 194
Philadelphia Phillies, 78
Pinelli, Babe, 101, 109, 112
Piniella, Lou, 178, 179, 182, 183, 186,
    189
Pittsburgh Pirates
    1959: 115–130, 194
    1960: 133–150, 194
    1975: 154
Plank, Eddie, 19, 20, 21
Podres, Johnny, 3
Polo Grounds (New York), 77, 78,
    80, 84, 97, 154
Powers, Mike, 19

Quinn, Jack, 63, 66, 67, 70

Randolph, Willie, 179
Reese, Pee Wee, 81, 83, 84, 85, 86, 88,
    101–102, 103, 104, 107
Remy, Jerry, 174, 177, 180, 183, 188,
    189
Rice, Del, 125
Rice, Jim, 156, 176, 177, 180, 182,
    183, 188, 189
Rice, Sam, 46, 48, 50, 51, 53, 54
Richardson, Bobby, 134–135, 139, 143,
    145, 146–147
Richmond, John, 123
Rickey, Branch, 14
Rigney, Bill, 88
Rivers, Mickey, 178, 179, 180, 182,
    185, 186, 188
Rizzuto, Phil, 101
Robertson, Charley, 107–108, 123
Robinson, Brooks, 84, 178
Robinson, Jackie, 78, 81, 85, 86, 101,
    102, 104, 106, 108
Rommel, Eddie, 70, 71
Root, Charlie, 62, 65–66, 67, 70, 71, 72
Rose, Pete, 4, 158, 160, 163, 167

Rossman, Claude, 12, 13, 14, 16, 17,
    19, 21
Roush, Edd, 31
Ruel, Muddy, 46, 50, 51, 53, 54, 55,
    56, 57–58
Ruffing, Red, 173
Ruth, Babe, 9, 62, 98, 103, 104, 116,
    136, 154, 173

St. Louis Browns, 8
Schaefer, Germany, 12, 13, 16, 21
Schmidt, Boss, 11, 12, 13, 14, 16
Schoendienst, Red, 117
Schofield, Dick ("Ducky"), 119, 122,
    123, 125, 128
Schreck, Ossie, 10, 13, 14, 16
Scott, George, 177, 182, 186, 188
Seybold, Socks, 11, 12, 14, 16
Shantz, Bobby, 141, 142, 143, 144, 145
Shean, Davy, 30, 32, 34, 35, 36, 39
Shibe Park (Philadelphia), 62, 63, 74,
    139, 154
Shore, Ernie, 123
Simmons, Al, 62, 65, 67, 70, 72, 73
Skinner, Bob, 119, 120, 122, 123, 124,
    135, 136, 139, 141, 145
Skowron, Bill ("Moose"), 101, 134,
    141, 143, 144, 145, 147
Slaughter, Enos, 100, 104, 107
Smith, Hal, 136, 138, 144, 145–146,
    147
Smith, Vinnie, 128
Snider, Duke, 3, 81, 83, 84, 85, 86, 87,
    102, 103, 104, 107
Spahn, Warren, 116, 117
Speaker, Tris, 154
Spencer, Jim, 183–185
Sportsman's Park (St. Louis), 154
Stafford, Bill, 141
Stanky, Eddie, 79–80, 81, 83, 84, 86,
    88, 101
Stanley, Bob, 186
Stanley, Fred, 184
Steinbrenner, George, 174, 185
Stengel, Casey, 99, 100–101, 133, 135,
    139–141, 143, 144, 145, 147
Stephenson, Riggs, 62, 66, 67, 70, 73,
    74
Stuart, Dick, 125, 134
Sukeforth, Clyde, 89
Sutter, Bruce, 17
Swoboda, Ron, 167

Tate, Benny, 53
Taylor, Tommy, 46, 48, 53
Taylor, Zack, 65, 67, 70
Terry, Bill, 47, 48, 49, 50, 51
Terry, Ralph, 146, 148, 150
Thomson, Bobby, 5, 80, 81, 83–84, 86, 88, 91, 94, 97
Thorpe, Jim, 5, 31, 32, 34, 36, 37–38, 39
Tiant, Luis, 157, 159, 160, 161, 162, 175
Tiger Stadium (Detroit), 153
Toney, Fred, 31–32, 33, 34, 35, 36, 37, 39
Torrez, Mike, 174, 177–178, 180, 183, 185, 186, 190
Turley, Bob, 138, 139

Vaughn, Jim (Hippo), 28, 29, 30, 31, 32, 34, 35, 36, 37, 38–39, 40
Virdon, Bill, 119, 122, 123, 125, 129, 136, 139, 141, 144, 145, 148

Waddell, Rube, 5, 8–9, 13–14, 15, 16, 17–19, 21, 22, 24
Walberg, Rube, 63, 70
Walker, Rube, 83, 85, 86
Washington Senators, 8, 22, 43–58, 194
Weeghman, Charles, 26, 40
Weeghman Park (Chicago), 26
Westrum, Wes, 79, 81, 84, 85, 88
White, Roy, 179, 182, 183

Williams, Cy, 27, 30, 32, 34, 35, 37, 39
Williams, Ted, 156
Willoughby, Jim, 162
Wilson, Art, 27, 29, 32, 34, 36, 37, 38–39, 40
Wilson, Hack, 48, 50, 51, 56, 57, 62, 65, 66, 67, 68, 70, 71, 72
Wiltse, George, 124
Wise, Rick, 168
Wolter, Harry, 29, 32, 34, 37
World Series, 25
    1919: 31
    1924: 43–58, 194
    1929: 61–74, 194
    1956: 97–112, 194
    1957: 116, 117
    1960: 133–150, 194
    1975: 154–170, 194
Wrigley Field (Chicago), 26, 63, 153

Yankee Stadium (New York), 97, 98–99, 154
Yastrzemski, Carl, 154, 156, 158, 159, 161, 162, 163, 166, 175–177, 180, 182, 183, 185, 188, 189–190
Young, Cy, 123
Youngs, Ross, 47, 48, 50, 51, 55, 56, 57

Zachary, Tom, 47
Zeider, Rollie, 27, 32, 34, 37
Zimmer, Don, 174, 177, 178, 183, 186, 188

PHOTO CREDITS

Boston Red Sox, 157, 161, 176; Detroit Tigers, 18, 22; courtesy of the National Baseball Hall of Fame and Museum, Inc., 10-11, 15, 28, 33, 52, 68-69, 90, 118; New York Yankees, 100, 181, 184, 187; Pittsburgh Pirates, 121, 137, 140, 143, 146; unless otherwise credited, photos are from the author's personal collection.